to PASTOR RON

MERRY CHRISTMAS

from

PEACE LUTHERAN CHURCH MEMBERS

JOE AND ELAINE MAHAFFIE

The Best of

BITS & PIECES

COMPILED AND EDITED BY
ARTHUR F. LENEHAN

THE ECONOMICS PRESS, INC.
12 DANIEL ROAD
FAIRFIELD, NEW JERSEY 07004-2565

© 1994 by The Economics Press, Inc.

All rights reserved in all countries. No part of this book may be reproduced, stored in a retrieval system, or transmitted, in any form or by any means, electronic, mechanical, photocopying, recording, or otherwise without the prior written permission of the copyright holder.

Printed in the United States of America.

The Best of Bits & Pieces
Library of Congress Catalog Card Number: 94-72406

The Best of Bits & Pieces
ISBN 0-910187-08-8

The Economics Press, Inc.
Fairfield, New Jersey

The Best of Bits & Pieces is dedicated to John L. Beckley, who founded The Economics Press in his garage in Montclair, New Jersey, over 40 years ago.

The 200-plus employee-owners of The Economics Press, now an internationally known and respected publisher of high-quality training and development programs, will be forever grateful to "Mr. B" for his wit, wisdom, leadership, and "mixture of horse sense and common sense about working with people."

Preface

OR YEARS, readers of *Bits & Pieces* have been asking that we publish a collection of the little essays, anecdotes, jokes, proverbs, and one-liners that appear every four weeks in our pocket-size magazine. The requests have come from all over the world. That's because we mail *Bits & Pieces* to readers in more than 100 countries.

How many readers? We don't know. We *do* know that circulation is more than 250,000, and that most of these subscribers pass their copies along to others. We would be willing to bet that readership is well over 1,000,000.

When we say that *Bits & Pieces* gets passed around, one exception comes to mind. We met a retired corporate executive in Florida recently who said he had always kept his large collection of *Bits & Pieces* issues locked in his desk so that associates wouldn't know the source of the illustrative stories he used in his speeches.

It would have been simple to take this loyal but selfish fellow's collection and put it in book form, but we felt that a representative selection would be more manageable and meaningful. It proved to be a hard task.

From the beginning, *Bits & Pieces* has been aimed at executives, managers, and supervisors in the business world. Advice on how to deal with people in the workplace has been its mainstay. But through the years the magazine has developed a broader appeal with bits of advice about getting along with people outside the workplace and within the family. Gentle humor has broadened the magazine's appeal even more. Humor has also served to make the advice more palatable. But perhaps the best reason for this little magazine's popularity can be found in a comment that we frequently get from readers: "*Bits & Pieces* gives me a lift."

Actually, the title of this book should be *The Best of Bits & Pieces Plus*. The "plus" represents the fact that some of the material that follows is from *Bits & Pieces'* younger companion publication, *Leadership*. *Leadership* was first published nearly 10 years ago in response to readers of *Bits & Pieces* who wanted more of what they had come to like in the latter. The two publications are virtual clones that are mailed two weeks apart.

To produce these two little magazines, we have picked flowers from many gardens (thank you Mark Twain, Benjamin Franklin, Abraham Lincoln, and others). But we have also cultivated our own sources.

We have tried to do so with an economy of words—the way Count Basie produced great piano music by hitting an economy of notes. And, although we may never achieve it, our goal has always been to write prose the way Robert Frost wrote poetry—beginning in delight and ending in wisdom.

This book is the result. While we present it as "the best" of our efforts, we're well aware that some of our readers may have other ideas.

If you have a favorite essay, story, proverb, or bit of humor that you remember reading in *Bits & Pieces* that you feel belongs here, drop us a line and let us know. It might lead to *More of the Best of Bits & Pieces*.

Arthur F. Lenehan
Editor

Acknowledgments

$\mathcal{A}$S EDITOR OF *Bits & Pieces* and *Leadership*, I am grateful to a group of associates at The Economics Press to whom I have circulated the initial text of each issue. This group includes the management team, starting with our publisher, John Beckley; Michael LoRusso, Alan Yohalem, and Robert Kleinmanns. Others whose critiques I have valued are writers and editors here. They include Robert Guder, whose comments would make a book in itself—a funny one; Phil Hall, Geoff Steck, Diane Cody, Linda Bullock, Muriel Friedman, Anne Marie Rovetto, Susan Cooper, and Jonathan Hotz. My special thanks go to Dorothy Edler, who puts the words I bang out on my old typewriter into a computer, straightening out my grammar and punctuation as she goes.

A word of thanks is also due our artists and graphics group: Charles Palminteri, Tom Freet, Elisa Greuter, Roni Palmisano, and Debbie McIntyre.

Arthur F. Lenehan
Fairfield, N.J.

What a good thing Adam had—when he said a good thing, he knew nobody had said it before him.

MARK TWAIN

CONTENTS

❖ ❖ ❖ ADVERSITY

If you're feeling low, don't despair. The sun has a sinking spell every night, but it comes back up every morning.

ENTERTAINER DOLLY PARTON once said that if you want the rainbow, you have to put up with the rain.

Rainbows are beautiful, but Dolly is right—it takes both rain and sunshine to create one. It's the same with life. In most lives there are dark and bright spots; there's joy and sorrow. The few people who have never known adversity invariably don't have lives that are as rich and satisfying as those who have. If you can handle it, adversity makes you stronger. It also makes you a kinder and more empathetic person. At the end of a life without adversity, it's hard to find a rainbow.

We cannot control the tragic things that happen to us, but we can control the way we face up to them.

❖ ❖ ❖ ADVERTISING

AN ELEPHANT met a lion in the jungle and asked, "Why do you roar so much?"

"I am king of the beasts," said the lion, "and I roar to advertise that fact."

1

A rabbit overheard this exchange and was duly impressed. The next day the rabbit encountered a fox and he decided to try the lion's strategy. Unfortunately, when he tried to roar, it came out sounding like a tiny squeak. The squeak attracted the attention of the fox and the fox immediately pounced on the rabbit and ate him.

Clearly, it does not pay to advertise unless you have the goods.

When someone stops advertising,
*   someone stops selling.*
When someone stops selling,
*   someone stops buying.*
When someone stops buying,
*   someone stops making.*
When someone stops making,
*   someone stops working.*
When someone stops working,
*   someone stops earning.*
When someone stops earning,
*   everything stops.*

A TROUBLED BUSINESSMAN once said to P. T. Barnum, "I have tried advertising and did not succeed, yet I have a good product."

"My friend," said Barnum, "there may be exceptions to a general rule. But how did you advertise?"

"I put it in a weekly newspaper three times," said the man, "and paid a dollar and a half for it."

"Sir," said Barnum, "advertising is like learning—a little is a dangerous thing."

❖ ❖ ❖ ADVICE

IN HIS *Creed for Optimists*, Christian D. Larsen tells you how you can be *somebody*.

> Be so strong that nothing can disturb your peace of mind. Talk health, happiness, and prosperity to every person you meet. Make all your friends feel there is something in them. Look at the sunny side of everything. Think only of the best, work only for the best, and expect only the best. Be as enthusiastic about the success of others as you are about your own. Forget the mistakes of the past and press on to the greater achievements of the future. Give everyone a smile. Spend so much time improving yourself that you have no time left to criticize others. Be too big for worry and too noble for anger.

I used to call Count Basie one of my lawyers. He would give such beautiful advice and he would phrase that advice into these little sayings. One I'll always remember pertains to the time my husband and I broke up. Basie said, "It's just like a toothache. It hurts now, but if you take that tooth out, you'll miss it but you'll feel better."

ELLA FITZGERALD

The advice your child rejected is now being given to your grandchild.

AGE ❖ ❖ ❖

As we grow older, our bodies get shorter and our anecdotes get longer.

A FRIEND used an interesting expression the other day. He referred to "the gentleness of age." The trials and tribulations of life bring each of us our share of bitter disappointments. Yet they also leave behind a greater sense of understanding, tolerance, and sympathy for others—something we never felt to the same extent when we were younger. That's the "gentleness of age."

I'm at the age where my back goes out more than I do.

PHYLLIS DILLER

No matter how old some people get, they never seem to lose their attractiveness. They merely move it from their faces to their hearts.

You can't help getting older, but you don't have to get old.

GEORGE BURNS

WHEN someone told 89-year-old poet Dorothy Duncan that she had lived a full life, she responded tartly, "Don't you past tense me!"

In our youth-oriented society the message often sent to older adults is that their usefulness ends at 65—if not sooner. Many like

Dorothy Duncan recognize this for the nonsense it is and go right on leading productive lives.

Artist Pablo Picasso was still producing drawings at 90—and his painting became more innovative with the years.

Pianist Artur Rubinstein gave one of his greatest recitals at 89.

Actress Jessica Tandy won an Academy Award at 80 for her performance in *Driving Miss Daisy*.

Congressman Claude Pepper of Florida was still actively championing the rights of the elderly and the poor at 88.

Environmentalist Marjory Stoneman Douglas, credited with saving the Everglades, was still fighting for the cause at age 100.

Happy, productive older people don't necessarily refuse to retire from their jobs. But they do refuse to retire from life.

The young and the old have all the answers. Those in between are stuck with the questions.

ONE OF THE THINGS that impresses most of us as we grow older is how many nice people there are in this world. Even people we used to find annoying or downright irritating don't seem to bother us so much. We discover that many of the ones we didn't particularly like really aren't as bad as we thought.

Maybe we're a little smarter than we used to be. We have begun to understand why prickly pears are prickly, and make allowance for it. Other people appreciate the change in the way we react to them, and it makes them more friendly toward us.

Taking this tack makes for smoother sailing. Life becomes friendlier and more enjoyable. You learn to forgive and forget.

Those who don't learn this miss out on the warmth and friendships they might enjoy.

The test of a people is how it behaves toward the old. It is easy to love children. Even tyrants and dictators make a point of being fond of children. But the affection and care for the old, the incurable, the helpless, are the true gold mines of a culture.

ABRAHAM HESCHEL

AMBITION ❖ ❖ ❖

Never judge anyone until you discover what they *would like to be*, as well as what they are.

WHEN HARRY AND ADA MAE DAY had Sandra, their first child, they had to travel 200 miles to El Paso, Texas, for the delivery. They brought Sandra home to their ranch on the Arizona/New Mexico border, where life was not easy.

Their little adobe home had no electricity or running water. There was no school within driving distance. With such limited resources, anyone would have thought that Sandra's future was not bright.

When Sandra was four, her mother began her education at home. She looked on it as a never-ending job, reading to Sandra hour after hour. Later, Sandra was sent to the best boarding schools the Days could afford because they wanted her to go on to college. The father, Harry, had been frustrated in his ambition to attend Stanford University. Harry's father died just before Harry was to enter Stanford and he had been forced to take over the ranch.

Sandra *did* go to Stanford, then on to law school, and eventually became the first female justice of the U.S. Supreme Court.

What causes someone like Sandra Day O'Connor to go so far? Intelligence and inner drive had a lot to do with it, but much of the credit must go to a set of determined parents. Harry and Ada Mae Day used every possible opportunity to enhance their daughter's education and prepare her for her role as an outstanding citizen.

A FRIEND'S GRANDFATHER came to America from Europe, and after being processed at Ellis Island, he went into a cafeteria in New York City to get something to eat. He sat down at an empty table and waited for someone to take his order. Of course, nobody did. Finally, a man with a tray full of food sat down opposite him and told him how things worked.

"Start at that end," he said, "and just go along and pick out what you want. At the other end they'll tell you how much you have to pay for it."

"I soon learned that's how everything works in America," Grandpa told our friend. "Life is a cafeteria here. You can get anything you want as long as you're willing to pay the price. You can even get success. But you'll never get it if you wait for someone to bring it to you. You have to get up and get it yourself."

❖ ❖ ❖ APPEARANCE

ABRAHAM LINCOLN was well aware of the fact that he was not a handsome man. When told that someone had called him "two-faced," he said, "If I was two-faced, would I be wearing this one?"

The leader of a visiting group once introduced a member of the group as an active and earnest friend of the President and as an artist "who has been good enough to paint and present to our league rooms a most beautiful portrait of yourself."

President Lincoln shook the artist's hand and said, "I presume, sir, in painting your beautiful portrait, you took your idea of me from my principles and not from my person."

When both were practicing law, Edwin Stanton referred to Lincoln on at least one occasion as a "gorilla," and other associates were disappointed at his homely appearance when they first met him.

Lincoln found this understandable and he never let such criticism alter his feelings about other people. As a lawyer, he learned to respect Edwin Stanton's mind and when he became president, Lincoln did not hesitate to ask Stanton to join his cabinet as Secretary of War.

Stanton and everyone else who came to know him well soon forgot about Lincoln's looks and became aware of his inner beauty. When Lincoln was shot, Stanton looked down on the rugged face of the President and said through tears, "There lies the greatest ruler of men the world has ever seen." Lincoln's forbearance, patience, and love conquered in the end.

DAVID LLOYD GEORGE, the British statesman, was a short man.

Someone once gave him a bumbling introduction, pointing out that the prime minister was a big man in many ways, but a small one in stature.

Lloyd George replied, "In North Wales, where I come from, we measure a man from his chin up. Here, you evidently measure him from his chin down."

❖ ❖ ❖ APPRECIATION

A SALESWOMAN caught in a traffic jam looked out of her car window into the window of a music store where a piano was on display. At it sat a man who, by the rapt expression on his face, was playing some music that he obviously loved.

The saleswoman couldn't hear a note, but she was fascinated as she watched him play. When he finished, she caught his eye, held her hands up and applauded, mouthing the words, *Bravo! Bravo!*

The pianist stood up and bowed deeply. Then they both laughed, the traffic light changed, and the saleswoman drove off, pleased with herself, humankind, and life in general.

LOOK FOR THE GOOD IN LIFE and you will find it. That may seem like a cliché these days, but it is just as true now as it ever was.

One man who believed it was Edward L. Kramer of St. Louis, Missouri. Back in 1948 Kramer sought to teach this principle to his three children.

He asked them to deliberately look each day for the good in at least three people, people to whom they could be thankful. "It can be in your playmates, your teachers—anyone with whom you come in contact," he told them.

Each evening, after dinner, Kramer would sit down with his children and ask them for an accounting of the good they had found in people that day. Then postcards expressing their appreciation were mailed to those individuals.

At first the children found the job difficult. But as they began to train themselves to look for acts of kindness, trust, and generosity, they found it easier and easier to do.

After a time their thoughtfulness, their gratitude, was

returned to them tenfold in the warmth and thankfulness of the people who received the cards. The family found themselves mailing so many they designed their own card. It was patterned after the yellow telegram of Western Union. They called it a Thank-U-Gram.

During the next 15 years or so, Kramer supplied people all over the country with millions of Thank-U-Grams. Such diverse people as President Eisenhower, Robert Frost, Leonard Bernstein, Bob Hope, Walt Disney, Henry Ford II, Jack Benny, and thousands upon thousands of others, both great and small, used Kramer's Thank-U-Grams—an idea that grew out of a father's desire to teach his children a moral principle about life.

WE can't think of anybody who lived a more hectic life than Theodore Roosevelt. But even during his campaign trips, when the demands upon him might have excused him from thinking of others, he always left his private train to stop and thank the engineer and fireman for a safe and comfortable trip. It only took a minute or two of his time, but it earned him friends for life.

"Glad-hander—just good politics," you might say. But it's good human relations too. And it's so easy to do.

On the way to work you can thank total strangers with a gesture of the hand, a nod of the head, a grateful glance. Thank the driver who stops to allow you to cross the street. Thank the person who holds a door for you. Thank everyone for everything. It works wonders.

ASSUMPTIONS ❖ ❖ ❖

AFTER PHYSICIST RICHARD FEYNMAN won a Nobel Prize for his work, he visited his old high school. While there, he decided to look up his records.

He was surprised to find that his grades were not as good as he had remembered them. And he got a kick out of the fact that his IQ was 124, not much above average.

Dr. Feynman said that winning the Nobel Prize was one thing, but to win it with an IQ of only 124 was really something. Most of us would agree because we all assume that the winners of Nobel prizes have exceptionally high IQs.

If Feynman had known he was really just a bit above average in the IQ department, would he have had the audacity to launch the unique and creative research experiments that would eventually win him the greatest recognition the scientific community can give?

Perhaps not. Maybe the knowledge that he was a cut above average, but not in the genius category, would have influenced what he tried to achieve. After all, from childhood most of us have been led to believe that ordinary people don't accomplish extraordinary feats.

Most of us fall short of our potential because of little things we know or assume about ourselves. And the most self-defeating assumption of all is that we are just like everyone else.

❖ ❖ ❖ **ATTITUDE**

You can often change things if you just change your attitude.

A TRAVELER nearing a great city asked a man seated by the wayside, "What are the people like in the city?"

"How were the people where you came from?"

"A terrible lot," the traveler responded. "Mean, untrustworthy, detestable in all respects."

"Ah," said the sage, "you will find them the same in the city ahead."

Scarcely was the first traveler gone when another one stopped and also inquired about the people in the city before him. Again the old man asked about the people in the place the traveler had left.

"They were fine people; honest, industrious, and generous to a fault. I was sorry to leave," declared the second traveler.

Responded the wise one: "So you will find them in the city ahead."

There is little difference in people, but that little difference makes a big difference. The little difference is attitude. The big difference is whether it is positive or negative.

CLEMENT STONE

AUTHORITY ❖ ❖ ❖

WHEN Christian Herter was governor of Massachusetts, he was running hard for a second term in office. One day, after a busy morning chasing votes (and no lunch) he arrived at a church barbecue. It was late afternoon and Herter was famished.

As Herter moved down the serving line, he held out his plate to the woman serving chicken. She put a piece on his plate and turned to the next person in line.

"Excuse me," Governor Herter said, "do you mind if I have another piece of chicken?"

"Sorry," the woman told him. "I'm supposed to give one piece of chicken to each person."

"But I'm starved," the governor said.

"Sorry," the woman said again. "Only one to a customer."

Governor Herter was a modest and unassuming man, but he decided that this time he would throw a little weight around.

"Do you know who I am?" he said. "I am the governor of this state."

"Do you know who *I* am?" the woman said. "I'm the lady in charge of the chicken. Move along, mister."

––––––

A SUPERVISOR was trying to encourage his people to act on their own initiative. He received a call from a worker whom he had already given full authority to proceed on his own. "Shall I finish this job or go on to the next one?" the fellow asked.

"Yes," replied the supervisor and hung up.

A few minutes later the telephone rang again. "Do you mean yes I should finish the old job, or yes I should begin the new one?"

"No," answered the supervisor and hung up again.

––––––

DURING WORLD WAR II John Eisenhower was an aide on the staff of his father, General Dwight D. Eisenhower. On one occasion, the general gave him a message to deliver to a colonel on the front lines.

The young lieutenant found the colonel and told him, "My dad says to watch your right flank."

"Really?" said the puzzled officer. "And what does your mommy say?"

––––––

BEAUTY ❖ ❖ ❖

To have beauty is to have only that, but to have goodness is to be beautiful too.

SAPPHO

AN EASTERNER on his first trip west, traveling on a bus tour, was unmoved by the scenery, scoffed at the Grand Canyon, yawned at the Petrified Forest and the Painted Desert, and had no interest at all in Yellowstone Park.

When the bus driver had had too much of this carping and indifference, he finally turned to the fellow and said quietly, "Mister, when you haven't got it inside, you can't see it outside."

The best and most beautiful things in the world cannot be seen or even touched. They must be felt with the heart.

HELEN KELLER

BEGINNINGS & ENDINGS ❖ ❖ ❖

THERE WERE two ships in a harbor. One was setting out on a journey. The other was coming home to port. Everyone cheered the ship going out, but the incoming ship was scarcely noticed.

To this a wise man said: "Do not rejoice over a ship setting out to sea, for you cannot know what terrible storms it may encounter. Rather, rejoice over the ship that has safely reached port and brings its passengers home in peace."

This is the way of the world: When a child is born, all rejoice; when someone dies, all weep. We should do the opposite. For no one can tell what trials and travails await a newborn child, but when mortals die in peace, we should rejoice, for they have completed a long journey, and there is no greater boon than to leave this world with the imperishable crown of a good name.

Adapted from
the *Talmud*

FAILURES come to all of us. No matter how hard we try, sometimes things will go wrong. Success is usually gained through long striving, though occasionally it is reached with less difficulty. After all, the harder we have to work for the attainment of an object, the more we appreciate it when it is in our possession. Do not be discouraged because of failures; begin over. Throughout the entire world people are beginning over; there is not a household but has learned the lesson. There is rebuilding done at all times of the year—a pulling down of half-finished plans, a ripping out of false stitches, and a new start being made. Take fresh courage, and try again, no matter how hard it may be.

Break a spider's web, and she will set to work immediately to repair the damage; rob a beehive, and the little occupants will go on making cells and gathering fresh stores of honey; brush down an anthill, and the busy little ants will go to cleaning out the rubbish and rebuilding the demolished house at once. It is always creditable to be willing to begin over.

IDA SCOTT TAYLOR

A DOCTOR who had devoted his life to helping the poor lived over a liquor store in the ghetto section of a large city. In front of the liquor store was a sign reading *Dr. Williams Is Upstairs.*

When he died, he had no relatives and he left no money for his burial. He had never asked for payment from anyone he had ever treated. Friends and patients scraped enough money together to bury the good doctor, but they had no money for a tombstone. It appeared that his grave was going to be unmarked until someone came up with a wonderful suggestion. They took the sign from in front of the liquor store and nailed it to a post over his grave. It made a lovely epitaph: *Dr. Williams Is Upstairs.*

BREVITY ❖ ❖ ❖

The most difficult thing for people to say in 25 words or less is good-bye.

Nothing can be said after 20 minutes that amounts to anything.

WHENEVER WE LISTEN to all those long-winded speeches at political conventions, we recall our favorite political speech. It was by Calvin Coolidge.

President Coolidge was returning to Washington from an American Legion convention in Omaha, when his train stopped for coal and water at a small town. The stop had been publicized and 2500 people were waiting when the train pulled into the station. An aide informed Coolidge about the crowd and the President walked back to the rear platform. When he appeared, the crowd applauded. Mrs. Coolidge was then introduced and got an even bigger ovation.

The local master of ceremonies then took center stage. "Now folks, keep quiet," he said. "I want absolute silence. The President is about to address us." A hush descended. "All right," the man said, "Mr. President, you may speak now."

At that point there was a hiss of air as the train brakes were released, and the train slowly began to move out of the station. The President smiled, waved to the crowd, and said, "Good-bye."

❖ ❖ ❖ BROTHERHOOD

ONE DAY, Turgenev, the Russian writer, met a beggar who asked him for alms. "I felt in all my pockets," he says, "but there was nothing there. The beggar waited, and his outstretched hand twitched and trembled slightly. Embarrassed and confused, I seized his dirty hand and pressed it. 'Do not be angry with me, brother,' I said, 'I have nothing with me.' The beggar raised his bloodshot eyes and smiled, 'You called me brother,' he said, 'that was indeed a gift.'"

— ARCHER WALLACE

If you want to see brotherhood in action, if you want to see sharing, helpfulness, cooperation, and togetherness, just watch a bunch of high-school kids taking a final examination. That is the time when there is no question of race, creed, or color. There is only one question. "Who's got the answer?"

SAM LEVENSON

BUSINESS ❖ ❖ ❖

WITH COLLEGE EXPENSES IN MIND, a working mother recently made some investments for her young daughter. One of the things she did was buy stock in a bank in her daughter's name.

Two months later, the bank sent the following form letter to her daughter:

"It has come to our attention that you recently became an owner of our stock. May we suggest that you recommend our bank and its services to your friends and business associates?"

The woman replied, "My daughter, who is 19 months old, has asked me to thank you for your letter and to explain that she has no business associates, only a half dozen acquaintances, and just two of what she regards as real friends, a cat named Misty and a dog named Woof. Unfortunately, she pulled Misty's tail and bit Woof's ear yesterday, leaving her at the moment without friends *or* business associates. However, she graciously extends her cordial greetings and says she is looking forward to receiving your next quarterly financial report."

———

TWO PARTNERS in a car rental firm fell upon hard times. Business was bad, money was tight, and they couldn't agree on anything. They decided to meet for lunch at a nice restaurant and make some tough decisions.

One partner arrived late to find his colleague glassy-eyed. "You'll never guess what happened," said the latter. "I was sitting here when Lee Iacocca walked in! His party was late, so we struck up a conversation and I told him about our problem."

"What did he say?"

"Iacocca says we're doing it all wrong! We can't make money in the short-term rental business. Hertz and Avis will have us for lunch! Forget that and concentrate on longer-term personal auto leases. That's where the money is!"

"Well, if Iacocca says so, let's try."

And try they did. In six months they broke even. In a year they made a profit. And in three years they were the largest, most profitable auto leasing firm in the state.

One night the partner met Iacocca at a gala and thanked him for the advice. "I don't know what you're talking about," said Iacocca. "I don't know you or your partner. I never give business advice, and I've never been in that restaurant."

Shattered, the partner called his colleague. "I just met Lee Iacocca. He says he never gave you any advice. He never spoke to you. He doesn't even know who you are!"

"So?"

"So, you lied to me! Those ideas weren't Lee Iacocca's, they were all yours!"

There was a pause. "If you knew that three years ago, would you have gone along with me?"

The Jokesmith

❖ ❖ ❖ **CATS**

Of all God's creatures there is only one that cannot be made the slave of the lash. That one is the cat. If man could be crossed with the cat, it would improve man, but it would deteriorate the cat.

MARK TWAIN

Cats seem to operate on the principle that it never does any harm to ask for what you want.

Dogs come when they're called; cats take a message and get back to you.

MISSY DIZICK

CHANGE ❖ ❖ ❖

MARKETS CHANGE, tastes change, so the companies and the individuals who choose to compete in those markets must change.

But change is not always sudden and dramatic, and the changes that can do the most harm are those that we don't see coming. Consider the story of the frog that was dropped into a pan of hot water. The frog immediately reacted to the heat by jumping out of the pan.

Another frog was put into a pan of cold water on a stove. The burner beneath the pan was turned on low, then the heat was gradually increased so the temperature of the water rose only a degree at a time. Change was occurring, but because it was gradual the frog accepted it and stayed in the pan and was boiled.

In a way, we're all in the same pan. We react immediately to dramatic changes, but we run the risk of getting cooked if we fail to notice the little, slow changes occurring around us.

❖ ❖ ❖ CHARACTER

Reputation grows like a mushroom; character like an oak.

Character is what you are in the dark.

How people play the game shows something of their characters. How they lose shows all of it.

Ability may get you to the top, but only character will keep you there.

The real judges of your character aren't your neighbors, your relatives, or even the people you play bridge with. The folks who really know you are waiters, waitresses, and clerks.

KATHERINE PIPER

❖ ❖ ❖ CHEER/CHEERFULNESS

Nothing is more beautiful than cheerfulness in an old face.

J.P. RICHTER

THE LATE MAURICE CHEVALIER was once asked how he managed to be so cheerful.

The entertainer admitted that even though he invariably

appeared to be cheerful, he didn't always feel that way. But he added, "When I sense an audience responding to the gaiety I am trying to give out, I feel gaiety coming back to me. It is like a boomerang—a little blessed boomerang. This works not only for the performer. It is a good game anybody can play.

"A man goes to his office," Chevalier went on. "He is grumpy, growls a greeting to his secretary. She may have awakened spirited and jaunty, but right away the ugliness is contagious. Or, in reverse, he comes in whistling. Maybe he has picked a flower from his garden for his buttonhole. He extends a merry greeting. It boomerangs. The office brightens.

"There are targets everywhere. Just take aim and let go with good cheer," said Chevalier. "The business of getting back something for what you give appeals to my practical French nature, especially when the something benefits you so much. It is what they call in business *a high rate of return.*"

There is no market for gloom. You cannot sell it. What the world wants, needs, and will buy is cheer.

THE NEXT TIME you're feeling sorry for yourself, do something nice for somebody. It will make you feel better.

The late Robert Updegraff, a prominent business consultant, tells a story about it in a book called *Try Giving Yourself Away* (Prentice Hall), which he wrote many years ago under the pen name of David Dunn.

"I remember sitting at breakfast one morning at a lunch counter near the South Station in Boston. Having arrived on the sleeper train from New York, and having been routed out of my berth before seven o'clock after a poor night's sleep, I was feeling very sorry for myself.

22

" 'What you have to accomplish in Boston today is too important to risk failure just because you feel grumpy,' I told myself sternly. 'You better start giving away . . . . But how can you give away sitting on a stool in a row of other grumpy night travelers before seven o'clock in the morning?' I said to myself.

"Then I looked at the salt and pepper. I recalled reading of some woman who said she was sure her husband loved her dearly—but he *never* thought to pass her the salt and pepper. I had noticed ever since how seldom anyone takes the trouble to pass them.

"I glanced up and down the counter. The only salt and pepper shakers in sight were directly in front of *me*. I had already seasoned my fried eggs, with no thought of my fellow diners. Now, picking up the shakers, I offered them to the man on my right.

" 'Perhaps you—and some of the other people down the line—can use these,' I said.

"He thanked me, seasoned his eggs, and passed the shakers on. Every person at the counter used them.

"That broke the ice. I got into a conversation with my neighbor, and the man next to him joined in. Before I knew it, everyone at the counter was talking, and presently we were all laughing and joking, eating breakfasts seasoned with salt, pepper, and good humor. And *I* had supplied the seasoning.

"By the time I had finished my breakfast, I was feeling positively cheerful. My mission in Boston that day worked out better than I thought possible."

———————————

CHILDREN ❖ ❖ ❖

If you want your children to turn out well, spend twice as much time with them, and half as much money on them.

ABIGAIL VAN BUREN

———————

TEACHER Debbie Moon's first graders were discussing a picture of a family. One little boy in the picture had different color hair than the other family members.

One child suggested that he was adopted and a little girl named Jocelynn Jay said, "I know all about adoptions because I'm adopted."

"What does it mean to be adopted?" asked another child.

"It means," said Jocelynn, "that you grew in your mother's heart instead of her tummy."

GEORGE DOLAN
Fort Worth Star-Telegram

———————

The only thing of value we can give kids is what *we are*, not what *we have*.

LEO BUSCAGLIA

———————

There are only two kinds of travel: first class and with children.

ROBERT BENCHLEY

———————

A TELEMARKETER called a home one day, and a small voice whispered, "Hello?"

"Hello! What's your name?"

Still whispering, the voice said, "Jimmy."

"How old are you, Jimmy?"

"I'm four."

"Good. Is your mother home?"

"Yes, but she's busy."

"Okay, is your father home?"

"He's busy too."

"I see, who else is there?"

"The police."

"The police? May I speak with one of them?"

"They're busy."

"Any other grown-ups there?"

"The firemen."

"May I speak with a fireman, please?"

"They're all busy."

"Jimmy, all those people in your house, and I can't talk with any of them? What are they doing?"

"Looking for me," whispered Jimmy.

The Jokesmith

———————

Show us a home with young children and we'll show you a home

where every pack of cards counts out at between 37 and 51.

BILL VAUGHAN

IF I HAD influence with the good fairy who is supposed to preside over the christening of all children, I should ask that her gift to each child in the world be a sense of wonder so indestructible that it would last throughout life, as an unfailing antidote against boredom and disenchantments of later years, the sterile preoccupation with things that are artificial, the alienation from our sources of strength.

RACHEL CARSON

COMMON SENSE ❖ ❖ ❖

Ten Points of Common Sense:

1. You cannot bring about prosperity by discouraging thrift.

2. You cannot strengthen the weak by weakening the strong.

3. You cannot help small men by tearing down big men.

4. You cannot help the poor by destroying the rich.

5. You cannot lift the wage earner by pulling down the wage payer.

6. You cannot keep out of trouble by spending more than your income.

7. You cannot further the brotherhood of man by inciting class hatred.

8. You cannot establish sound security on borrowed money.

9. You cannot build character and courage by taking away a man's initiative and independence.

10. You cannot help men permanently by doing for them what they could and should do for themselves.

WILLIAM J. H. BOETCKER

One of the great maladies of our time is the way sophistication seems to be valued above common sense.

NORMAN COUSINS

THERE IS an ancient tale about a king who wanted to pick the wisest man among his subjects to be his prime minister. When the search finally narrowed down to three men, he decided to put them to the supreme test.

Accordingly, he placed them together in a room in his palace. On the room door he had installed a lock that was the last word in mechanical ingenuity. The candidates were informed that whoever was able to open the door first would be appointed to the post of honor.

The three men immediately set themselves to the task. Two of them began at once to work out complicated mathematical formulas to discover the proper lock combination. The third man, however, just sat down in his chair, lost in thought. Finally, without bothering to put pen to paper, he got up, walked to the door, and turned the handle. The door opened to his touch. It had been unlocked all the time!

Mind your own business—and have plenty of it.

Tackle one job at a time.

Make decisions quickly, and don't fear the outcome.

Learn to delegate a part of your work and your responsibilities.

Don't stake too much on success.

Don't be afraid of failure.

Don't overvalue the unattainable.

Don't undervalue what you have.

Forget the people you don't like.

Keep both your sense of humor and your sense of proportion.

Forget yesterday. It is gone.

Don't dread tomorrow. It isn't here yet.

COMMUNICATION ❖ ❖ ❖

THE POWER of a successfully communicated thought is one of the greatest forces we know. But like the tango, it takes two to communicate. You can communicate a thought, but your thought may not be understood. In some cases, your thought may not even reach the proper target. That's why it pays to ask questions to make certain that people understand what you are saying. The great moviemaker Cecil B. DeMille would agree.

DeMille was making one of his great epic movies. He had six cameras at various points to pick up the overall action and five other cameras set up to film plot developments involving the major characters. The large cast had begun rehearsing the scene at 6 a.m. They went through it four times and now it was late afternoon. The sun was setting and there was just enough light to get the shot done. DeMille looked over the panorama, saw that all was right, and gave the command for action.

One hundred extras charged up the hill; another hundred came storming down the same hill to do mock battle. In another location Roman centurions lashed and shouted at 200 slaves who labored to move a huge stone monument toward its resting place.

Meanwhile the principal characters acted out, in close-up, their reactions to the battle on the hill. Their words were drowned out by the noise around them, but the dialogue was to be dubbed in later.

It took 15 minutes to complete the scene. When it was over, DeMille yelled, "Cut!" and turned to his assistant, all smiles. "That was great!" he said.

"It was, C.B.," the assistant yelled back. "It was fantastic! Everything went off perfectly!"

Enormously pleased, DeMille turned to face the head of his camera crew to find out if all the cameras had picked up what they had been assigned to film. He waved to the camera crew supervisor.

From the top of the hill, the camera supervisor waved back, raised his megaphone, and called out, "Ready when you are, C.B.!"

BACK IN THE 1920s an executive of the New York Telephone Company stopped in amazement one evening to observe a man in a tuxedo emerging from a manhole at the corner of 42nd Street and Broadway.

The man turned out to be Burch Foraker, head of the Bell Telephone system in New York City. On that cold January night Foraker had come out of a theater and descended into the manhole as though it was part of his job.

Was there a crisis? Was he worried about some serious difficulty in the system? Nothing of the sort.

"I knew there were a couple of my cable splicers working down there, so I just dropped in on 'em to have a little chat," said Foraker.

In time, Foraker became known as the "man of 10,000 friends" due in part to the fact that he made a habit of visiting his men at their work. It was his way of showing that he considered their jobs important.

Good managers and executives show their associates that they respect their ability. They display a genuine interest in what they are doing. They drop in, chat a bit, ask a few questions, and perhaps make a useful suggestion. Try it. It never does any harm and it can do a lot of good.

PRESIDENT FRANKLIN D. ROOSEVELT was a great talker and when he got together with any of his advisers, they found it difficult to break in with a word.

One who succeeded was Cordell Hull, Secretary of State. He was a frequent luncheon guest but he always had a snack before his arrival. Then when the President stopped talking to eat, Hull would speak his piece.

WHATEVER YOUR MESSAGE is, keep it simple.

A fellow came into a diner and said to the waitress, "I want a club sandwich with one slice of white bread, one of pumpernickel, and one of whole wheat, toasted medium. Put the bacon and cheese on the bottom layer, the chicken, lettuce, and tomato on the top layer. Put mayonnaise on each layer. Trim the crusts and cut it up into fourths, with a sliced pickle on each part, and a toothpick to hold each part together. Got it?"

"Gotcha," said the waitress. Then she yelled into the kitchen, "One club—for an *architect*. I'll be right in with the plans."

WE ALL need somebody to talk to. It would be good if we talked to each other—not just pitter-patter, but real *talk*. We shouldn't be so afraid, because most people really like this contact; that you show you are vulnerable makes *them* free to be vulnerable too. It's so much easier to be together when we drop our masks.

LIV ULLMAN

❖ ❖ ❖ COMMUNISM

THE TRANSITION from communism to democracy and capitalism has been frustrating and painful. Some people even long for the security of the days when the Union of Soviet Socialist Republics held sway and life held fewer uncertainties.

Our eastern European correspondent explained why:

"Things ran much more smoothly in those days," he said. "Here in Hungary we were producing little dwarfs made of clay, like Snow White and the Seven Dwarfs, which were placed in gardens for decoration. We used to export these little figures to Bulgaria and the Bulgarians would send us little chicks. We would feed these chicks our good Hungarian grain until they became big chickens. We would then export the chickens to Czechoslovakia and they would send us little piglets. The piglets were fed our good Hungarian corn until they became big, fat pigs. We would send the pigs to Romania and they would send us little calves. The calves would be fed our good Hungarian grain until they became big cows and bulls. When they were big enough, we would export them to the Soviet Union and the U.S.S.R. would send back clay so we could make more little dwarfs."

COMPASSION ❖ ❖ ❖

PRESIDENT ABRAHAM LINCOLN often visited hospitals to talk with wounded soldiers during the Civil War. Once, doctors pointed out a young soldier who was near death and Lincoln went over to his bedside.

"Is there anything I can do for you?" asked the President.

The soldier obviously didn't recognize Lincoln, and with some effort he was able to whisper, "Would you please write a letter to my mother?"

A pen and paper were provided and the President carefully began to write down what the young man was able to say:

"My dearest mother, I was badly hurt while doing my duty. I'm afraid I'm not going to recover. Don't grieve too much for me, please. Kiss Mary and John for me. May God bless you and father."

The soldier was too weak to continue, so Lincoln signed the letter for him and added, "Written for your son by Abraham Lincoln."

The young man asked to see the note and was astonished when he discovered who had written it. "Are you really the President?" he asked.

"Yes, I am," Lincoln replied quietly. Then he asked if there was anything else he could do.

"Would you please hold my hand?" the soldier asked. "It will help to see me through to the end."

In the hushed room, the tall, gaunt President took the boy's hand in his and spoke quiet words of encouragement until death came.

❖ ❖ ❖   CONFIDENCE

THERE'S NOTHING LIKE SELF-CONFIDENCE. Talk-show host Larry King tells this story about baseball great Ty Cobb. When Cobb was 70, a reporter asked him, "What do you think you'd hit if you were playing these days?"

Cobb, who was a lifetime .367 hitter, said, "About .290, maybe .300."

The reporter said, "That's because of the travel, the night games, the artificial turf, and all the new pitches like the slider, right?"

"No," said Cobb, "it's because I'm 70."

A MAN stopped to watch a Little League baseball game. He asked one of the youngsters what the score was.

"We're behind 18 to nothing," was the answer.

"Well," said the man, "I must say you don't look discouraged."

"Discouraged?" the boy said, puzzled. "Why should we be discouraged? We haven't come to bat yet."

GOLFER Arnold Palmer has never flaunted his success. Although he has won hundreds of trophies and awards, the only trophy in his office is a battered little cup that he got for his first professional win at the Canadian Open in 1955.

In addition to the cup, he has a lone framed plaque on the wall. The plaque tells you why he has been successful on and off the golf course. It reads:

If you think you are beaten, you are.
If you think you dare not, you don't.
If you'd like to win but think you can't,
It's almost certain that you won't.
Life's battles don't always go
To the stronger woman or man,
But sooner or later, those who win
Are those who think they can.

CONGRESS ❖ ❖ ❖

NEWLY ELECTED MEMBERS of the U.S. Congress would do well to listen to the advice British Prime Minister Benjamin Disraeli gave to a new member of Parliament.

"For the first six months," said Disraeli, "you should only listen and not become involved in the debate."

"But my colleagues will wonder why I do not speak!" the fledgling member protested.

"Better they should wonder why you do not, than why you do!" replied Disraeli.

In Congress, after all is said and done, more is said than done.

NEW JERSEY REPRESENTATIVE Bill Hughes liked to tell the story of a newly elected congressman holding his first town meeting. In the question-and-answer portion of the meeting, a voter complained about the lack of snow removal from her street following a recent storm.

"With all due respect, ma'am, this is a local problem," said the congressman. "Have you told your mayor about this?"

"No, I didn't," the woman replied. "I didn't want to start that high up."

In 1884, John Allen of Tupelo, Mississippi, ran for a seat in Congress and his opponent was a General Tucker, who had served with the Army of the Confederacy during the Civil War. Allen had served as a private.

In one debate, the General pointed out the contrast between his rank and Allen's.

"I admit I was only a private," replied Allen. "In fact, I was a sentry who stood guard over the general when he slept. And now all you fellows who were generals, and had privates standing guard over you, vote for General Tucker. But all you boys who were privates and stood guard over the generals, vote for Private John Allen."

They did, and Allen was a congressman for the next 16 years.

❖ ❖ ❖ **CONSCIENCE**

A YOUNG ACCOUNTANT was offered some easy money—$50,000—to do some things with the figures for the books of a client—things that made him uneasy. What he was being asked to do wasn't clearly illegal, but it didn't seem quite ethical either.

That night he talked the matter over with his mother and asked her what she thought.

The mother paused for a moment and then said, "You know, Tom, when I come to wake you in the morning I shake hard and you don't stir. I shake you even harder and you give a little moan. And finally I shake you as hard as I can and you open one sleepy eye. I'd hate to come in every morning and find you awake."

The young man turned down the job and has been sleeping soundly since.

––––––––––––––

YOUR CONSCIENCE is a little triangle in your heart. It acts like a pinwheel. When you're good it does not rotate. When you're bad, it turns around and the corners hurt a lot. If you keep on being bad, the corners eventually wear off, and when the little triangle spins around it doesn't hurt anymore.

CONSULTANTS ❖ ❖ ❖

ONCE UPON A TIME there was a little town that had a great surplus of cats. A task force was appointed to find out why. It discovered that the population surge was the doing of a particularly virile tomcat. The task force recommended that the cat be neutered by the local vet.

The recommendation was followed. All was normal for two years, then there was again an unwelcome surge in the cat population. The task force was called back to work and found that the former tomcat had spent the two years at Harvard Business School and was now back in town as a consultant.

CONVERSATION ❖ ❖ ❖

WE HEARD about a fellow who has a surefire line to get a conversation going with the person next to him at a dinner party. He looks at whatever piece of jewelry a woman is wearing and says, "Tell me the story of how you got that." He claims he has never been bored by the reply.

––––––––––––––

A bore talks mostly in the first person, a gossip in the third, and a good conversationalist in the second.

THE REAL ART OF CONVERSATION is not only to say the right thing in the right place but to leave unsaid the wrong thing at the tempting moment.

DOROTHY NEVELL

A BRITISH BUSINESSWOMAN was having tea with a visiting American businessman and he said, "This tea is great! I wish we could get tea like this in America."

The woman replied, "But, my dear sir, we sent you a whole boatload once, and you dumped it into the harbor."

❖ ❖ ❖ **COSTS**

WHETHER you're putting a new addition on your house, installing new machinery in a factory, or erecting a new office building, the problem of cost overruns always seems to crop up.

The ancient Greeks knew how to handle it. They would have bidders submit estimates of the cost of constructing a public building. The winning bidder would then have to turn over his property and assets to a magistrate until the job was completed. If the job was finished at or below the estimate, the bidder was awarded a commendation in his honor. If the work was up to 25 percent over budget, the state paid. But if costs went beyond 25 percent, assets equal to the overrun were taken from the contractor.

COURAGE ❖ ❖ ❖

The courage of life is often a less dramatic spectacle than the courage of a final moment, but it is no less than a magnificent mixture of triumph and tragedy. People do what they must—in spite of personal consequences, in spite of obstacles and dangers and pressures—and that is the basis of all human morality.

JOHN F. KENNEDY

HEROIC DECISIONS are not made by cowards, as this story attests:

A little girl was near death, victim of a disease from which her younger brother had miraculously recovered two years before. Her only chance to live was a blood transfusion from someone who had previously conquered the sickness. The doctor explained the situation to Tommy, the five-year-old brother, and asked if he would be willing to give his blood to his sister, Kathy.

The boy took a deep breath, thought for a moment, then drew himself up and said, "Yes, I'll do it if it will save my sister."

As the transfusion progressed one could see the vitality returning to the wan figure of the little girl. Tommy smiled when he observed this, but then, with trembling lips he said something startling.

"Will I begin to die right away?" he asked.

The doctor realized immediately what Tommy's hesitation had meant earlier. In giving blood to his sister, he thought he was giving up his life! In one brief moment he had displayed more courage than most of us can muster in a lifetime. He had made an heroic decision!

Courage is resistance to fear, mastery of fear, not absence of fear.

MARK TWAIN

WHATEVER YOU DO, you need courage. Whatever course you decide upon, there is always someone to tell you that you are wrong. There are always difficulties arising that tempt you to believe your critics are right. To map out a course of action and follow it to an end requires some of the same courage that a soldier needs. Peace has its victories, but it takes brave men and women to win them.

RALPH WALDO EMERSON

❖ ❖ ❖ COURTESY

THOSE WHO SOW COURTESY reap friendship. When courtesy is expressed it increases the well-being of all concerned. People who attain greatness know its value.

Mark Twain did. Max Eastman, the writer, recalls being introduced to Twain at the height of his career. Eastman was only 11 years old. It wasn't at all necessary for a noted author to be courteous to a child, but Mark Twain was. He took the trouble to talk to the young Eastman, gravely inquiring about his schooling and other things. Max Eastman never forgot it.

There was a man named Frank Munsey, who built a fortune in the publishing business. One of his employees recalled that on the first day he went to work, he told Mr. Munsey that he was deaf in his right ear. In the 25 years they worked together, not once did Frank Munsey stand on that side of this man when he was talking to him. What a beautiful example of courtesy!

Scatter the seeds of courtesy about whenever you can. Some are bound to fall on fertile ground and you will grow in the eyes of others.

CREATIVITY ❖ ❖ ❖

THE CREATIVE SPIRIT (Dutton), written by Daniel Goleman, Paul Kaufman, and Michael Ray, offers dramatic examples of how you can put creativity to work in whatever you do.

During periods of great change, answers don't last very long, but a *question* is worth a lot. A creative life is a continued quest, and good questions are useful guides. The most useful questions are open-ended; they allow a fresh, unanticipated answer to reveal itself.

These are the kinds of questions children aren't afraid to ask. They seem naive at first. But think how different our lives would be if certain questions were never asked. Jim Collins of Stanford's Graduate School of Business has compiled the following list of "questions of wonder":

Albert Einstein: What would a light wave look like to someone keeping pace with it?

Bill Bowerman (inventor of Nike shoes): What happens if I pour rubber into my waffle iron?

Fred Smith (founder of Federal Express): Why can't there be reliable overnight mail service?

Godfrey Hounsfield (inventor of the CAT scanner): Why can't we see in three dimensions what is inside a human body without cutting it open?

Masaru Ibuka (honorary chairman, Sony): Why don't we remove the recording function and speaker and put headphones in the recorder? (Result: the Sony Walkman.)

Here's a simple exercise you can do to develop your ability to ask questions that can produce radically new and unexpected ideas. Each day, for a week, take a few minutes to ask yourself a question that begins: "I wonder . . . ." Ask this question about a particular area of your life, such as the workplace. "I wonder what would happen if we divided the corporation into 12 smaller, autonomous companies?" It is essential not to censor yourself, no matter how impractical or outlandish the question sounds.

After you have had some practice doing this, try going public with your questions by posing them to friends or colleagues. Listen carefully to their responses. As in the story of the Emperor's New Clothes, you'll probably discover that your question reveals blind spots and assumptions that deserve to be challenged.

WHEN St. Petersburg, Russia, one of the most splendid and harmonious cities in Europe, was being laid out early in the 18th century, many large boulders brought by a glacier from Finland had to be removed.

One particularly large rock was in the path of one of the principal avenues that had been planned, and bids were solicited for its removal. The bids submitted were very high. This was understandable, because at that time modern equipment did not exist and there were no high-powered explosives. As officials pondered what to do, a peasant presented himself and offered to get rid of the boulder for a much lower price than those submitted by other bidders. Since they had nothing to lose, officials gave the job to the peasant.

The next morning he showed up with a crowd of other peasants carrying shovels. They began digging a huge hole next to the rock. The rock was propped up with timbers to prevent it from rolling into the hole. When the hole was deep enough, the timber props were removed and the rock dropped into the hole below the street level. It was then covered with dirt, and the excess dirt was carted away.

It's an early example of what creative thinking can do to solve a problem. The unsuccessful bidders only thought about moving the rock from one place to another on the city's surface. The peasant looked at the problem from another angle. He considered another dimension—up and down. He couldn't lift it up, so he put it underground.

A COLLEGE PROFESSOR was awarded a grant by a foundation to do scholarly work abroad. She had a problem, however. The grant came in the middle of the school year and she was unsuccessful in getting another professor to finish up the year with her class.

The professor came up with a solution. She told her class about the foundation grant and said she would make tape recordings of her remaining lectures and that the recordings would be played during regular class hours. The students could listen to the tapes and make notes.

The first class that was held under this arrangement was two days before the professor was to go abroad. When the class had started, the professor decided to check on how things were going. She quietly opened the rear door and peeked inside.

She saw and heard her tape recorder on her desk, delivering the lecture. But there were no students in the classroom. On their seats were 18 tape recorders, duplicating everything being said.

It happens all the time: Creativity inspires more creativity.

❖ ❖ ❖ CRITICISM

Criticism, like rain, should be gentle enough to nourish one's growth without destroying one's roots.

When weighing the faults of others, be careful not to put your thumb on the scale.

IT IS NOT the critic who counts, not the man who points out how the strong man stumbled or where the doer of deeds could have done better.

The credit belongs to the man who is actually in the arena; whose face is marred by dust and sweat and blood; who strives valiantly; who errs and comes short again and again; who knows the great enthusiasms, the great devotions, and spends himself in a worthy cause; who, at the best, knows in the end the triumph of high achievement; and who, at the worst, if he fails, at least fails while daring greatly, so that his place shall never be with those cold and timid souls who know neither victory nor defeat.

THEODORE ROOSEVELT

THE NEXT TIME you're being bombarded with criticism, remember Colonel George Washington Goethals, the man who successfully completed the Panama Canal.

He had problems enough with the geography and climate involved, yet he still had to endure the carping criticism of many busybodies back home who kept predicting that he would never complete the project. But he steadfastly stuck to the task and said nothing.

"Aren't you going to answer these critics?" an associate asked.

"In time," Goethals replied.

"How?"

"With the canal," Goethals said.

ACCORDING TO an ancient story, a man once approached Buddha and began to call him ugly names. Buddha listened quietly until the man ran out of epithets and had to pause for breath.

"If you offer something to a person and that person refuses it, to whom does it belong?" asked Buddha.

"It belongs, I suppose, to the one who offered it," the man said.

Then Buddha said, "The abuse and vile names you offer me, I refuse to accept."

The man turned and walked away.

If criticism had any real power to harm, the skunk would be extinct now.

FRED ALLEN

BEING CRITICIZED is not a problem if you develop a positive way of dealing with it. Winston Churchill had the following words of Abe Lincoln framed on the wall of his office: "I do the very best I can, I mean to keep going. If the end brings me out all right, then what is said against me won't matter. If I'm wrong, 10 angels swearing I was right won't make a difference."

A GUIDE AT Blarney Castle in Ireland was explaining to some visitors that his job was not always as pleasant as it seemed. He told them about a group of disgruntled tourists he had taken to the castle earlier in the week.

"These people were complaining about everything," he said. "They didn't like the weather, the food, their hotel accommodations, the prices, everything. Then to top it off, when we arrived at the castle, we found that the area around the Blarney Stone was roped off. Workers were making some kind of repairs."

"This is the last straw!" exclaimed one person who seemed to be the chief faultfinder in the group. "I've come all this way, and now I can't even kiss the Blarney Stone."

"Well, you know," the guide said, "according to legend, if you kiss someone who has kissed the stone, it's the same as kissing the stone itself."

"And I suppose you've kissed the stone," said the exasperated tourist.

"Better than that," replied the guide. "I've sat on it."

Keep away from people who try to belittle your ambitions. Small people always do that, but the really great make you feel that you, too, can become great.

MARK TWAIN

IN THE HEAT of an election a lot of people try to give what they don't have. They like to think they know everything about everything, and even when they don't know, they pretend that they do. You see it in letters to the editors of our newspapers. You hear it on radio and television.

President Abraham Lincoln was painfully aware of this. During the Civil War he was often denounced and criticized by people who wanted to give advice even though they had a minimum of knowledge. Their premises were often built on flimsy information. They offered wisdom they did not possess.

Lincoln handled it by telling the story of a backwoods traveler lost at night in an awesome thunderstorm. The traveler's horse had exhausted itself floundering through the mud on a flooded dirt road. Lightning streaked down out of the darkness, and thunder roared around the traveler as he stood in the road trying to figure his next move. At one point a bolt of lightning struck nearby, and a tremendous crash of thunder brought the traveler to his knees. Kneeling there in the mud, he cried out, "O Lord, if it's all the same to you, give us a little more light and a little less noise!"

CUSTOMER RELATIONS ❖ ❖ ❖

ON A STORMY NIGHT many years ago, an elderly man and his wife entered the lobby of a small hotel in Philadelphia. "All the big hotels are filled up," said the man. "Could you possibly give us a room here?"

The clerk explained that there were three conventions in town, and that there were no rooms to be had anywhere. "All our rooms are taken," he said, "but I can't send a nice couple like you out in the rain at one o'clock in the morning. Would you perhaps be willing to sleep in my room?"

The couple replied that they couldn't do that, but the clerk insisted. "Don't worry about me; I'll make out just fine," he told them.

Next morning, as he paid his bill, the elderly man said to the clerk, "You are the kind of manager who should be the boss of the best hotel in the United States. Maybe someday I'll build one for you."

The clerk looked at the man and his wife and smiled. The

three had a good laugh over the old man's little joke, and then the clerk helped them with their bags to the street.

Two years passed and the clerk had nearly forgotten the incident when he received a letter from the man. It recalled that night and enclosed a round-trip ticket to New York, asking the young man to pay them a visit.

In New York, the old man led him to the corner of Fifth Avenue and 34th Street and pointed to a great new building there, a palace of reddish stone, with turrets and watchtowers thrusting up into the sky.

"That," said the older man, "is the hotel I have just built for you to manage."

"You must be joking," the young man said.

"I most assuredly am not," said the older man, a sly smile playing around his mouth. The man's name was William Waldorf Astor. The hotel was the original Waldorf-Astoria and the young clerk, who became its first manager, was George C. Boldt.

ROBERT CONKLIN, author of *How to Get People to Do Things,* was on a plane when the captain announced over the intercom, "I want to apologize for the choppy ride this morning. We've been looking around for a little smooth air at some altitude, but it's hard to find. Sorry. But I hope you've enjoyed your breakfast. Thank you for flying with us."

After the plane landed and Conklin was getting off, a flight attendant again apologized. It made Conklin feel better.

"A few words of regret is a way of saying you care, a show of sensitivity to the ragged edges of another's emotions," Conklin points out in his book. "What difference does it make whose fault it was? Get it behind you with a little verbal peace offering. You'll make the other person feel better."

"The world keeps putting pebbles in your shoes. Walking along becomes more uncomfortable. It's nice to have someone come along and take a few out by saying things like this:

I'm sorry. You shouldn't have to put up with that.

I apologize. You were treated unfairly.

I don't blame you if you're upset. I regret that it happened."

MAMIE ADAMS always went to a branch post office in her town because the postal employees there were friendly.

She went there to buy stamps just before Christmas one year and the lines were particularly long. Someone pointed out that there was no need to wait on line because there was a stamp machine in the lobby.

"I know," said Mamie, "but the machine won't ask me about my arthritis."

DIFFERENCES ❖ ❖ ❖

THE DIVERSITY among earth's creatures is mind-boggling. For example, there's variety in the flying ability of birds.

The tiny hummingbird, weighing only about a tenth of an ounce, can perform complicated twists and turns and can fly backward and upside down.

The flexibility of its shoulder joints allows it to move its wings forward and backward in a horizontal figure 8, beating them as many as 75 times per second, a maneuver that enables the hummingbird to hover near a flower while it drinks nectar from it. But the hummingbird can't soar or glide as some birds can, and its legs are so weak that it can't hop. It has to fly even to change positions on a twig.

On the other hand, the ostrich, at 300 pounds, the largest of birds, can't fly. But its legs are so strong that it can sprint at up to 50 miles an hour, taking strides of 12 to 15 feet.

The peregrine falcon, or duck hawk, is about the size of a crow, but it is the fastest creature on earth. It can dive after prey at more than 175 miles per hour.

These differences are small when compared with the differences among humans. People have an infinite variety of special qualities and talents. Managers and supervisors should keep this in mind. Each individual has his or her own unique gifts that can be used to make the workplace and the world a better place.

Three Minutes a Day
Vol. 27, Christopher Books

The first day of spring is one thing, and the first spring day is another. The difference between them is sometimes as great as a month.

HENRY VAN DYKE

❖ ❖ ❖ **DIPLOMACY**

To make a good salad is to be a brilliant diplomat. One must know exactly how much oil one must put with one's vinegar.

OSCAR WILDE

In 1886, Karl Benz drove his first automobile through the streets of Munich, Germany.

The machine angered the citizens, because it was noisy and scared the children and horses. Pressured by the citizens, the local officials established a speed limit for "horseless carriages" of 3½ miles an hour in the city limits and seven miles an hour outside.

Benz knew he could never develop a market for his car and compete against horses if he had to creep along at those speeds, so he invited the mayor of the town for a ride. The mayor accepted. Benz then arranged for a milkman to park his horse and wagon on a certain street and, as Benz and the mayor drove by, to whip up his old horse and pass them—and as he did so to give the German equivalent of the Bronx cheer.

The plan worked. The mayor was furious and demanded that Benz overtake the milk wagon. Benz apologized but said that because of the ridiculous speed law he was not permitted to go any faster. Very soon after that the law was changed.

Benz proved that the art of diplomacy is getting people to see things *your* way.

"Diplomacy is nothing but a lot of hot air," said a companion to French statesman Georges Clemenceau as they rode to a peace conference.

"All etiquette is hot air," said Clemenceau. "But that is what is in our automobile tires; notice how it eases the bumps."

❖ ❖ ❖ DISCIPLINE

THERE ONCE was a terrible storm and an enormous pile of mud and rocks was washed up against a house. Soon, a man began to shovel small portions of the pile into a wheelbarrow. Then he would trundle the load over to the other side of his property, which had been washed away by the rain.

A friend came along, watched for a while, then said, "Jim, don't you realize that's too big a job for you?"

"Well," said the man, "I don't have enough money to have somebody come in here with a bulldozer, and while I'll admit it looks like too big a job for me, I'm not ready to admit that I can't do it without giving it a try."

Here was a man who didn't waste time worrying about the size of a job or his ability to finish it. He went ahead and started it. That's the first thing any of us should do if we want to whittle any job down to our size.

Writer Charles Swindoll has some good advice for all of us when we find ourselves facing a task that seems insurmountable.

Don't focus on the whole enchilada, he suggests, take the job in bite-size chunks. Even the most courageous can be overwhelmed by looking at what has to be done in its entirety.

If you're running in a 26-mile marathon, remember that every mile is run one step at a time. If you are writing a book, do it one page at a time. If you're trying to master a new language, try it one word at a time. There are 365 days in the average year. Divide any project by 365 and you'll find that no job is all that intimidating.

All it takes is discipline—daily discipline, not annual discipline.

DOCTORS ✦ ✦ ✦

Said Dr. Charles W. Mayo, founder of the famous Mayo Clinic:

"When I am your doctor, I try to imagine the kind of doctor I'd like if I were you. Then I try to be that kind of doctor."

Not a bad rule in any kind of job.

OLIVER GOLDSMITH'S fame rests principally on his talent as a great writer. But early in his life he was also a physician whose compassion for the sick and suffering went far beyond professional concern.

One day he was called to attend a very poor patient. Sick as the patient was, the doctor saw that he had need of more than medicine. Taking all the money he had with him, Goldsmith put it into a large pill box and wrote on the label: *To be taken as occasion requires.*

NORMAN VINCENT PEALE once asked a physician friend why he had become a doctor. The physician told him this story:

As a small boy he lived with his parents in a rural district of Kansas. In winter, the countryside lay under deep drifted snow and it was difficult to travel from the family farm to town and back.

One winter when he was about seven years old, his little sister got sick, ran a high fever, and became delirious. The little girl was near death by the time his father got a message over the nearly impassable roads and the doctor finally arrived. The doctor treated her and remained for 24 hours until the crisis passed. During that time the whole household was in anguish. No one had a minute's sleep.

Finally the little boy saw the doctor walk across the room

and put his hands on the shoulders of his father and mother, and heard him say to them, "By the grace of God, I am happy to tell you that little Mary will get well." The boy could see the faces of his parents. He had never seen them so lighted up, so wonderfully happy, so beautiful.

"Right at that moment," said Peale's physician friend, "I decided I was going to be a doctor, so I could say things like that to people that would bring that light to their eyes, that joy to their faces."

A medical student spent his summer vacation working as a butcher in the daytime and a hospital orderly in the evenings. Both jobs, of course, involved wearing a white smock.

One evening he was instructed to wheel a patient on a stretcher into surgery. The patient looked up at the student and let out an unearthly scream. "My God!" he cried, "it's my butcher!"

PIANIST ARTUR RUBINSTEIN, loquacious in eight languages, once told this story on himself:

Some years ago he was assailed by a stubborn case of hoarseness. The newspapers were full of reports about smoking and cancer; so he decided to consult a throat specialist. "I searched his face for a clue during the 30-minute examination," Rubinstein said, "but it was expressionless. He told me to come back the next day. I went home full of fears, and I didn't sleep that night."

The next day there was another long examination and again an ominous silence.

"Tell me," the pianist exclaimed. "I can stand the truth. I've lived a full, rich life. What's wrong with me?"

The physician said, "You talk too much."

ECONOMISTS ❖ ❖ ❖

WILLIAM FERGUSON, chairman of Nynex Corporation, once told this story about Albert Einstein in heaven:

Einstein was having difficulty finding people on his intellectual level to talk to, so one day he decided to stand at the pearly gates and ask people who entered what their IQ was. Before very long he was having a lot of success guessing what people did for a living on the basis of their level of intelligence.

For instance, a woman was ushered through the gates and in response to Einstein's question, said she had an IQ of 190. "Why, you must be a physicist," Einstein said. "Indeed I am," said the woman.

"I'd love to chat with you about the progress being made in nuclear fusion and in superconductivity, as well as what's going on in space," said Einstein. "Please wait over there."

He stopped a man who was entering the gates, and the man told him his IQ was 140. "You must be a physician, probably a surgeon," said Einstein. His guess was right. "Wonderful," said Einstein. "I want to talk to you about the latest organ transplant techniques and their effects on life expectancy. Can you wait a few moments until we can get together?"

Another man walked in and told Einstein he had an IQ of 75. "Is that so?" said Einstein. "So what do you think is going to happen with interest rates?"

❖ ❖ ❖ EDUCATION/LEARNING

We must view young people not as empty bottles to be filled, but as candles to be lit.

ROBERT H. SHAFFER

WE DON'T KNOW who wrote this little verse. It's undoubtedly aimed at teachers, but it could apply to anyone.

You never know when someone
May catch a dream from you.
You never know when a little word
Or something you may do
May open up the windows
Of a mind that seeks the light . . .
The way you live may not matter at all,
But you never know, it might.

AN ENGLISH PROFESSOR was flicking around the TV dial looking for something suitable for his son to watch. He found a rodeo and he and his son began watching it.

"Wow! Look at them bowlegged cowboys!" exclaimed the son at one point.

The professor was horrified with this improper use of language and he vowed then and there to begin schooling his son in English each evening, with a particular emphasis on the works of Shakespeare.

Two years later, he was again flicking the TV dial when he

came upon another rodeo. After watching for a few minutes, his son said, "What manner of men are these who wear their pants in parentheses?"

A FRIEND once asked Isidor I. Rabi, a Nobel Prize winner in physics, how he became a scientist.

Rabi replied that every day after school his mother would talk to him about his school day. She wasn't so much interested in what he had learned that day, but she always inquired, "Did you ask a good question today?"

"Asking good questions," Rabi said, "made me become a scientist."

The young make the mistake of thinking that education can take the place of experience; the old, that experience can take the place of education.

A FATHER and his small son were out walking one afternoon when the youngster asked how the electricity went through the wires stretched between the telephone poles.

"Don't know," said the father. "Never knew much about electricity."

A few blocks farther on the boy asked what caused lightning and thunder.

"To tell the truth," said the father, "I never exactly understood that myself."

The boy continued to ask questions throughout the walk, none of which the father could explain. Finally, as they were nearing home, the boy asked, "Pop, I hope you don't mind my asking so many questions . . . ."

"Of course not," replied the father. "How else are you going to learn?"

Sooner or later, of course, unless the father seeks the answers, the boy will stop asking questions. That would be unfortunate. Curiosity and the desire to learn should be encouraged and nurtured.

Parents who want their children to do well in school but who don't respect learning are deluding themselves. Not many children will be motivated to do it on their own.

The same is true in business. Managers or supervisors must set the example for those under them. If they have stopped learning and growing, they will be hard put to inspire their subordinates to do so, no matter how much they may pretend to encourage it.

———————

GREEK MATHEMATICIAN Euclid was engaged to teach geometry to a boy who was the heir to the Egyptian throne. The prince proved to be a poor student who balked at learning a system of logic that required him to prove so many elementary theorems before he could move on.

"Is there no simpler way you can get to the point?" he asked. "Surely the crown prince should not be expected to concern himself with such minutiae."

"Sire," responded Euclid, giving teachers through the ages that unforgettable phrase, "there is no royal road to learning."

———————

If you give a man a fish, he will eat once.
If you teach a man to fish, he will eat for the rest of his
*   life.*
If you are thinking a year ahead, sow seed.
If you are thinking 10 years ahead, educate the people.
By sowing seed, you will harvest once.

By planting a tree, you will harvest tenfold.
By educating the people you will harvest one
* hundredfold.*

KUANTZU

IN ANCIENT TIMES a king decided to find and honor the greatest person among his subjects. A man of wealth and property was singled out. Another was praised for his healing powers; another for his wisdom and knowledge of the law. Still another was lauded for his business acumen. Many other successful people were brought back to the palace, and it became evident that the task of choosing the greatest would be difficult.

Finally, the last candidate stood before the king. It was a woman. Her hair was white. Her eyes shone with the light of knowledge, understanding, and love.

"Who is this?" asked the king. "What has she done?"

"You have seen and heard all the others," said the king's aide. "This is their teacher."

The people applauded and the king came down from his throne to honor her.

ENTHUSIASM ❖ ❖ ❖

It is a mark of intelligence, no matter what you are doing, to have a good time doing it.

What the world needs is more people who will apply to their jobs the same enthusiasm for getting ahead as they display in traffic.

If you could give your son or daughter only one gift, let it be *enthusiasm*.

❖ ❖ ❖ **EXAGGERATION**

A MAN called his dentist for an appointment. "I've got a tremendous cavity!" he said.

When the man got into the dentist's chair, the dentist peered into his mouth and said, "Oh, that doesn't seem to be much of a cavity. We can take care of that with a small filling."

"Really?" said the man. "When I stick my tongue into it, it feels like it's huge."

The dentist smiled. "It's natural for the tongue to exaggerate, don't you think?" he said.

❖ ❖ ❖ **EXPERIENCE**

Experience is a comb that nature gives us when we are bald.

CHINESE PROVERB

A clay pot sitting in the sun will always be a clay pot. It has to go through the white heat of the furnace to become porcelain.

MILDRED WITTE STRUVEN

Experience is knowing a lot of things you shouldn't do.

WILLIAM S. KNUDSEN

It's what you learn after you know it all that counts.

JOHN WOODEN

FAILURE ❖ ❖ ❖

Failure should be our teacher, not our undertaker. Failure is delay, not defeat. It is a temporary detour, not a dead-end street.

THE EARLY LIVES of celebrated personalities reveal that some of them suffered painful discouragement from their teachers, judges, or peers.

Many of them were told they would never make it, or that they simply didn't have the necessary talent. But they wouldn't listen. They remained firm in following their own beliefs.

Consider some of these "failures":

Woody Allen, Academy Award-winning writer/producer/director, flunked motion picture production at New York University and the City College of New York and failed English at N.Y.U.

Malcolm Forbes, the late editor-in-chief of *Forbes* magazine, one of the largest business publications in the world, did not make the staff of *The Princetonian*, the school newspaper at Princeton University.

Leon Uris, author, flunked high school English three times.

Liv Ullman, two-time Academy Award nominee for Best

Actress, failed an audition for the state theater school in Norway. The judges told her she had no talent.

For all of us who will fail at one thing or another, take heart in one fact. In baseball, you can fail two out of three times at the plate and still make a few million dollars a year.

MILTON SNAVELY HERSHEY, the epitome of the American success story, knew about failure. As a boy, he went to work as a printer's apprentice. It didn't work out. Then he became an apprentice confectioner, where he fared better.

For five years he learned his trade and in 1876, at age 19, he moved to Philadelphia to start his own confectionery business. He worked hard for six years, but finally had to give up. He moved to Denver to work for another candy company.

Then he tried again. He and his father started a candy company in Chicago. It failed. They went to New Orleans, where another venture failed. New York was next. It was another failure.

But Milton Snavely Hershey learned from his mistakes. He learned that failure isn't fatal. He learned that obstacles can be stepping-stones. He learned that you never fail until you stop trying. Along the way he learned many tricks of the confection trade and came up with some new ones because he was constantly experimenting with new formulas and processes.

He began anew, opening the Lancaster Caramel Company in Pennsylvania in time for the Christmas trade. It was a success. Near the end of the century he was able to sell the company for a million dollars and embark on his greatest adventure.

Armed with money and new methods for processing milk chocolate that he had developed, he perfected the Hershey's Milk Chocolate bar and other products. In 1903, he began building a factory that became the world's largest chocolate manufacturing plant. He planned and built a town around the factory where people would be happy to live and raise their families.

In 1909 Hershey and his wife, Catherine, established the Milton Hershey School to provide a home and education for needy orphans. The Hersheys were unable to have children of their own and in 1918 he turned over the bulk of his fortune—99 percent of his personal wealth—to the M.S. Hershey Foundation, which supports the school.

A "failure" with little book learning, Milton Snavely Hershey became an inventor, entrepreneur, industrialist, philanthropist, and humanitarian. When he died in 1945 at age 88, his name was known throughout the world.

THE CALIFORNIA COAST was shrouded in fog that fourth of July morning in 1952. Twenty-one miles to the west on Catalina Island a 34-year-old woman waded into the water and began swimming toward California, determined to be the first woman to do so. Her name was Florence Chadwick and she had already been the first woman to swim the English Channel in both directions.

The water was numbing cold that July morning and the fog was so thick she could hardly see the boats in her own party. Millions were watching on national television. Several times sharks, which had gotten too close, had to be driven away with rifles to protect the lone figure in the water. As the hours ticked off she swam on. Fatigue had never been her big problem in these swims—it was the bone-chilling cold of the water.

More than 15 hours later, numbed with the cold, she asked to be taken out. She couldn't go on. Her mother and her trainer alongside in the boat told her they were near land. They urged her not to quit. But when she looked toward the California coast, all she could see was dense fog.

She had been pulled out only a half mile from the California coast! Later she was to reflect that she had been licked not by fatigue or even the cold—the fog had defeated her because it obscured her goal.

It was the only time Florence Chadwick ever quit. Two months later she swam that same channel, and again fog obscured her view, but this time she swam with her faith intact— somewhere *behind* that fog was land. Not only was she the first woman to swim the Catalina Channel, but she beat the men's record by some two hours!

❖ ❖ ❖ **FEAR**

WHEN YOU FEAR that the worst will happen, your own thoughts may help to bring it about. "Fear," a writer once said, "is the wrong use of imagination. It is anticipating the worst, not the best that can happen."

A salesman, driving on a lonely country road one dark and rainy night, had a flat. He opened the trunk—no lug wrench. The light from a farmhouse could be seen dimly up the road.

He set out on foot through the driving rain. Surely the farmer would have a lug wrench he could borrow, he thought. Of course, it was late at night—the farmer would be asleep in his warm, dry bed. Maybe he wouldn't answer the door. And even if he did, he'd be angry at being awakened in the middle of the night.

The salesman, picking his way blindly in the dark, stumbled on. By now his shoes and clothing were soaked. Even if the farmer did answer his knock, he would probably shout something like, "What's the big idea waking me up at this hour!"

This thought made the salesman angry. What right did that farmer have to refuse him the loan of a lug wrench? After all, here he was stranded in the middle of nowhere, soaked to the skin. The farmer was a selfish clod—no doubt about that!

The salesman finally reached the house, and banged loudly on the door. A light went on inside, and a window opened above. "Who is it?" a voice called out.

"You know darn well who it is," yelled the salesman, his face white with anger. "It's me! You can keep your blasted lug wrench. I wouldn't borrow it now if you had the last one on earth!"

Two caterpillars were crawling across the grass when a butterfly flew over them. They looked up, and one nudged the other and said: "You couldn't get me up in one of those things for a million dollars!"

A BACKWOODS FARMER, sitting on the steps of his tumbledown shack, was approached by a stranger who stopped for a drink of water.

"How's your wheat coming along?" asked the stranger.

"Didn't plant none."

"Really? I thought this was good wheat country."

"Afraid it wouldn't rain."

"Oh. Well, how's your corn crop?"

"Ain't got none," said the farmer.

"Didn't you plant any corn, either?"

"Nope, 'fraid of corn blight."

"For heaven's sake," said the stranger. "What did you plant?"

"Nothin'," said the farmer. "I just played it safe."

Anyone who has to make decisions cannot escape the tension, the emotional strain, involved. Nor can they "just play it safe" by avoiding decisions. Inability to cope with this basic fact of life has stopped many people short of their real potential.

♦ ♦ ♦ **FRIENDS/FRIENDSHIP**

You can make more friends in two months by becoming really interested in other people than you can in two years by trying to get other people interested in you.

DALE CARNEGIE

READER PHILIP W. HOPKINS once sent us a copy of a lovely thought he discovered on the wall of his doctor's office. It is called *What Is a Friend?* and is attributed to C. Raymond Beran.

Friends are people with whom you dare to be yourself. Your soul can be naked with them. They ask you to put·on nothing, only to be what you are. They do not want you to be better or worse. When you are with them, you feel like a prisoner feels who has been declared innocent. You do not have to be on your guard. You can say what you think, as long as it is genuinely you. Friends understand those contradictions in your nature that lead others to misjudge you. With them you breathe freely. You can avow your little vanities and envies and hates and vicious sparks, your meannesses and absurdities, and in opening them up to friends, they are lost, dissolved on the white ocean of their loyalty.

They understand. You do not have to be careful. You can abuse them, neglect them, tolerate them. Best of all, you can keep still with them. It does not matter. They like you. They understand. You can weep with them, sing with them, laugh with them, pray with them. Through it all—and underneath—they see, know, and love you.

What is a friend? Just one, I repeat, with whom you dare to be yourself.

Treat your friends as you do your paintings—place them in the best light.

JENNIE JEROME CHURCHILL

ALL OF US would like to have old friends. But have you ever stopped to think that old friends are not made in a hurry? If you would like to have such friends in the years to come, you had better start making new friends now. Sturdy friends, like sturdy beams, take time to season.

Go at this matter thoughtfully. Select persons you feel pretty sure could be the kind of friends you can prize in later years. Then start the gentle, gradual seasoning process.

How? Ralph Waldo Emerson gave us the answer. *The only way to have a friend is to be a friend.*

The reason dogs have so many friends is because they wag their tails and not their tongues.

DOUGLAS E. LURTON, who was a brilliant magazine editor and writer of motivational books decades ago, helped many people succeed in business and in life. He always advised them, among other things, to make as many friends as possible.

Once he even worked out a seven-day plan to win friends. He promised all who would follow it that they would not only have more friends at the end of a week, but that they would have a more pleasant week than they had ever known.

On the first day write a letter—write to an old friend or a new acquaintance. Make it a friendly, chatty, personal letter.

On the second day smile at every acquaintance you greet on the street or at work. And try to say a few words of praise to at least one person.

On the third day say something kind to every close associate you see.

On the fourth day call up someone you have just met and would like to know better and extend an invitation to lunch.

On the fifth day find someone who is not very popular and pay a lot of attention to him or her.

On the sixth day carry on a conversation with a stranger—a waiter, a waitress, a bus driver, a cab driver, or a train conductor. If possible, praise something that person has done.

On the seventh day encourage two people to talk about themselves. Say little about yourself. Get the others to talk.

All this may seem calculating, but something like it is necessary for most of us because we're reserved and that is a hindrance to making friends.

Friendship is like a bank account. You can't continue to draw on it without making deposits.

THE MOST PRECIOUS THING anyone can have is the goodwill of others. It is something as fragile as an orchid and as beautiful; as precious as a gold nugget and as hard to find; as powerful as a great turbine and as hard to build; as wonderful as youth and as hard to keep.

AMOS PARRISH

Treat your friends like family and your family like friends.

A BRITISH PUBLICATION once offered a prize for the best definition of a friend.

Among the thousands of answers received were the following: "One who multiplies joys, divides grief, and whose honesty is inviolable." "One who understands our silence." "A volume of sympathy bound in cloth." "A watch that beats true for all time and never runs down." The winning definition read: "A friend is the one who comes in when the whole world has gone out."

IN A LITTLE LEAGUE GAME several years ago the Royals were playing the Tigers and a Royal batter hit a drive that the Tiger right fielder made no attempt to catch.

At the end of the inning, the coach asked the boy, *"How come?"* The boy opened his glove to show a caterpillar he had picked up in the field.

"If I caught that ball," said the boy, "my new friend would have been killed."

ONE DAY a sophomore at Amherst College took a pair of shoes to be repaired to a shop run by a man named Jim Lucey. Lucey started a conversation with the shy young man and they became friends. The student stopped in frequently at the shop.

The student went on to become a lawyer and with the help of Jim Lucey he found an office in Northampton, Mass., not far from Lucey's shop. Their friendship grew and the young lawyer frequently dropped by the shop to talk to Lucey and other men who gathered there. He soon gained the respect of the group and before long they began urging him to run for political office in Northampton. A few years later, he was elected mayor.

That was the first step up the political ladder. Before long, the young man was elected to the state legislature in Boston and finally, Massachusetts voters made him governor.

In this office, he attracted the attention of national politicians and at the next national convention, the governor's name was put on the ticket for vice president.

His party won the election, but within three years, the President was fatally stricken, and in August of 1923, the former Amherst student was sworn in to the highest office in the land.

Several years later, a mail carrier delivered a letter to Jim Lucey's shoe shop in Northampton. The old shoemaker noticed that the return address on the envelope read, *The White House,* and his hands trembled as he opened it. There, on *White House* stationery, were these words:

My dear Mr. Lucey:

Not often do I see you or write to you, but I want you to know that if it were not for you I should not be here. I want to tell you how much I love you. Do not work too much now, and try to enjoy yourself in your well-earned hour of age.

Yours sincerely,

Calvin Coolidge

FUTURE ❖ ❖ ❖

The future seems to me no unified dream but a mince pie, long in the baking, never quite done.

E.B. WHITE

"NOTHING IS DONE," journalist Lincoln Steffens once wrote. "Everything in the world remains to be done—or done over. The greatest picture is not yet painted. The greatest play isn't written. The greatest poem is unsung."

Nothing is perfect, we can add. There's no perfect airline. There's no perfect government. There's no perfect law.

Faucets still drip, as one did years ago in the Steffens household. As he and his seven-year-old son tried to fix it, Steffens had to admit that his generation could not make a fit faucet.

"But," said Steffens, referring to his son, "*he* may. There's a job for him and his generation in the plumbing business, and in every other business.

"Teach your children," Steffens urged, "that nothing is done, finally and right; that nothing is known, positively and completely; that the world is theirs—all of it!"

Don't worry about what's ahead. Just go as far as you can go—from there you can see farther.

THERE is a kind of spider that skillfully lays a large number of eggs in the bark of a tree and proceeds to disguise them with her web. After a period, the baby spiders hatch, and the mother spider, with no thought of herself, goes about the business of finding food for her babies. When the baby spiders are strong enough to catch their own food, the exhausted mother dies . . . . The life of the baby spiders depends on the sacrifice and death of their mother.

In the same sense, the prosperity of a future generation in our world depends on the sacrifices made by the current generation.

Nothing comes free. Nothing is accidental. The more you dig, the deeper the hole, and the deeper the hole, the more water in the well. The child plucks the fruit from a tree the grandparent planted. If there is no tree, there is nothing for the child to pick.

If an entire generation thinks only of itself, what will be left? Even if we are not around to pick the fruit, we have the responsibility to plant the trees. Sacrifice is the ultimate form of altruism.

KIM WOO-CHOONG
Every Street Is Paved with Gold
William Morrow & Co.

Some people make the future; most wait for the future to make them.

♦   ♦   ♦   **GAMBLING**

An Easterner who walked into a Western saloon was amazed to see a dog sitting at a table playing poker with three men. "Can that dog really read cards?" he asked.

"Yeah, but he ain't much of a player," said one of the men. "Whenever he gets a good hand he wags his tail."

A FAMILY GROUP took great-grandmother to a racetrack for the first time.

71

She placed a $2 bet—another first—on a long shot whose name appealed to her. Her horse won and paid 25 to 1. As the clerk at the cashier's window handed the woman her winnings, she admonished him, "I hope this will be a lesson to you, young man!"

A GAMBLER at a Las Vegas roulette wheel was playing number 11. Unfortunately, he was having very little luck, but he was persistent. Long after midnight he was still at it. Most of the other players had left.

Finally, down to his last chips, he decided to take one more chance on number 11. It was then that he heard an unearthly voice whisper in his ear, "Put it on 16." The gambler wheeled around. There was no one near. Aside from himself and the yawning croupier, there wasn't a soul in sight. Puzzled, but impressed, the man shifted his remaining stake to number 16. The wheel spun and finally stopped—on 16! As he was about to rake in his chips, the voice spoke again. "Let it ride."

He did and won again.

By now the man was beside himself with excitement. Before touching the chips, he waited for the voice. He was not disappointed. "Put the whole pile on 22," it commanded. The gambler quickly did so.

The wheel spun again. As it slowed down, the silver ball hovered on the very edge of 22, then skittered out into the green zero.

"Oh, darn!" said the voice.

❖ ❖ ❖ **GENEROSITY**

Blessed are those who give without remembering and take without forgetting.

ELIZABETH BIBESCO

A MONK who was traveling in the mountains found a precious stone in a stream. The next day he met another traveler who was hungry, and the monk opened his bag to share his food. The hungry traveler saw the precious stone in the monk's bag, admired it, and asked the monk to give it to him. The monk did so without hesitation.

The traveler left, rejoicing in his good fortune. He knew the jewel was worth enough to give him security for the rest of his life.

But a few days later he came back searching for the monk. When he found him, he returned the stone and said, "I have been thinking. I know how valuable this stone is, but I give it back to you in the hope that you can give me something much more precious. If you can, give me what you have within you that enabled you to give me the stone."

ROBERTO DE VINCENZO, the great Argentine golfer, once won a tournament and, after receiving the check and smiling for the cameras, he went to the clubhouse and prepared to leave. Some time later, he walked alone to his car in the parking lot and was approached by a young woman. She congratulated him on his victory and then told him that her child was seriously ill and near death. She did not know how she could pay the doctor's bills and hospital expenses.

De Vincenzo was touched by her story, and he took out a pen and endorsed his winning check for payment to the woman. "Make some good days for the baby," he said as he pressed the check into her hand.

The next week he was having lunch in a country club when a Professional Golf Association official came to his table. "Some of the boys in the parking lot last week told me you met a young woman there after you won that tournament." De Vincenzo nodded. "Well," said the official, "I have news for you. She's a phony. She has no sick baby. She's not even married. She fleeced you, my friend."

"You mean there is no baby who is dying?" said De Vincenzo.

"That's right," said the official.

"That's the best news I've heard all week," De Vincenzo said.

GETTING ALONG ❖ ❖ ❖

TWO PEOPLE had adjoining farms. One raised wheat and had children and large dogs. The other raised sheep.

The sheep farmer was in a quandary because the dogs next door were running into his pastures and frightening the sheep. He spoke to his neighbor but the forays continued. He thought about taking the neighbor to court. He even thought about poisoning the dogs. Then one day he found a solution.

Some new lambs were born and the sheep farmer gave each of his neighbor's children a lamb as a pet. They were delighted! Because of the pet lambs, the father could no longer let the dogs run amok. He restrained them and taught them to leave the lambs and the sheep alone . . . and everybody lived happily ever after.

TEN SUGGESTIONS FOR GETTING
ALONG BETTER WITH PEOPLE:

1. Guard your tongue. Say less than you think.

2. Make promises sparingly. Keep them faithfully.

3. Never let an opportunity pass to say a kind word.

4. Be interested in others, their pursuits, work, families.

5. Be cheerful. Don't dwell on minor aches and small disappointments.

6. Keep an open mind. Discuss but don't argue. Disagree without being disagreeable.

7. Discourage gossip. It's destructive.

8. Be careful of others' feelings.

9. Pay no attention to ill-natured remarks about you. Live so that nobody will believe them.

10. Don't be anxious about getting credit. Just do your best and be patient.

———————

A WOMAN lived with her husband and two children in a very small hut. Then her husband's parents lost their home and she had to take them into hers.

The coughing of the old folks and the crowding were unbearable. In desperation, she went to the village wise man, whom she knew had solved many, many problems. "What should I do?" she begged.

"Do you have a cow?" asked the wise man.

"Yes," she replied.

"Then bring her into the hut too. And come back and see me in a week," said the wise man.

A week later she was back. "This is unbearable," she said.

"Do you have any chickens?" asked the wise man.

"Yes," she replied. "What about them?"

"Bring them in the hut too," he said. "Then come back and see me in another week."

"You're utterly out of your mind," she said. Nevertheless, still awed by his reputation, she did as he asked.

A week later she returned. "This is absolutely impossible," she said. "Our home is a mess of chicken feathers, cow dung, and people."

"All right," said the wise man, "take out the chickens."

The next week she reported that without the chickens it was definitely better but still a miserable situation. "All right," said the wise man, "now take out the cow. That will settle your problem."

And it did. Without the chickens and cow to contend with, the woman, her husband, the children, and his two parents got along quite peacefully. Everything, you see, is relative. Sometimes we don't know how well off we really are.

THOMAS JEFFERSON was a man of exceptional ability. But there have been many other people with as much or more ability, who never received the acclaim the world gave to this man.

The reason is that Jefferson had more than ability. He had the gift of being able to see how he could please others, and he pleased them. How did he exert so much charm over everyone who met him? Even those who had doubts about him, who even disliked him and opposed him on occasion, became his friends. Why?

The answer is simple. *He made everyone feel important.*

When he was President, Mrs. Samuel Harrison Smith wrote something that gives us an illuminating example of how he accomplished this.

"He gave everyone an opportunity of talking," she said. "I recollect at one dinner there was a man who was silent and neglected. To him the President said, 'We are indebted to you, Mr. Collins. No one deserves more gratitude of the country.' He then described a very minor contribution Mr. Collins had made.

"Every eye turned to the guest, who honestly looked more astonished than anyone else in the room. He had been a mere cipher before. Now he had become a person of importance."

It's such a simple idea and one that all of us can use every day in our contact with others. All of us meet men and women daily who are starving for attention, yearning for importance. Give it to them and you'll win friends.

❖   ❖   ❖   **GIVING**

Of all the dear sights in the world, nothing is so beautiful as a child when it is giving something. Any small thing it gives. A child gives the world to you. It opens the world to you as if it were a book you'd never been able to read. But when a gift must be found, it is always some absurd little thing, pasted on crooked . . . an angel looking like a clown. A child has so little that it can give, because it never knows it has given you everything.

MARGARET LEE RUNBECK

You can give without loving, but you can't love without giving.

THE LITTLE SISTERS OF THE POOR were going from door to door in a French city, soliciting alms for old people.

One nun called at the house of a rich freethinker who said he would give 1,000 francs if she would have a glass of champagne with him.

It was an embarrassing situation for the nun, and she hesitated. But the hesitation was short—after all, 1,000 francs meant many loaves of bread.

A servant brought the bottle and poured, and the brave little nun emptied the glass. And then she said, "And now, sir, another glass, please, at the same price."

She got it.

THE MENNONITES consider it wrong to take pay for helping another human being. Instead they say, *"I will charge thee nothing but the promise that thee will help the next man thee finds in trouble."*

IN 1784 Benjamin Franklin wrote the following letter to a man named Benjamin Webb:

"Dear Sir: Your situation grieves me and I send you herewith a banknote for 10 louis d'or. I do not pretend to give such a sum; I only lend it to you. When you shall return to your country, you cannot fail of getting into some business that will in time enable you to pay all your debts.

"In that case, when you meet with another honest man in similar distress, you must pay me by lending the sum to him, enjoining him to discharge the debt by a like operation when he shall be able and shall meet with such another opportunity.

"I hope it may thus go through many hands before it meets with a knave that will stop its progress. This is a trick of mine for doing a deal of good with a little money. I am not rich enough to afford much in good works, and so am obliged to be cunning and make the most of a little.

"With best wishes for your future prosperity, I am, dear sir, your most obedient servant. B. Franklin."

To give without any reward, or any notice, has a special quality of its own.

ANNE MORROW LINDBERGH

MARIAN ANDERSON once performed at a concert in a small Nebraska college town. A student who was working her way through college was terribly disappointed when she could not get time off from her job at the local hotel to attend the concert.

The great contralto was staying at the hotel, and after the concert she entered the lobby and went to the desk to see if there were any messages. The student inquired about the concert and expressed her disappointment that she had not been there.

Marian Anderson stepped back, and there in the hotel lobby, unaccompanied, sang *Ave Maria* for the student.

---

*First, you believe in Santa Claus. Then you don't believe in Santa Claus. And before you know it, you **are** Santa Claus.*

The test of generosity is not how much you give, but how much you have left.

GOLF ❖ ❖ ❖

One of the quickest ways to meet new people is to pick up the wrong ball on a golf course.

A GOLFER who had been playing badly went to a psychiatrist who told him to relax by playing a round of golf without a ball.

"Do everything you would normally do, but use an imaginary ball," advised the psychiatrist.

The golfer tried it the next day. He stepped up on the first tee, imagined he got a 260-yard drive, made a fine approach shot to the green, then putted for a par.

The round went splendidly and as he approached the 18th hole, he met another golfer playing the same way—no ball. The other golfer had seen the same psychiatrist. They decided to play the last hole together and bet $10 on the outcome.

The first golfer swung at his imaginary ball and announced that it had gone 280 yards right down the middle of the fairway. The second golfer matched his drive.

The first fellow then took out his five-iron and after swinging at his imaginary ball, he exclaimed, "Look at that shot! It went right over the pin and the reverse spin on it brought it right back into the hole! I win."

"No you don't," said the second golfer. "You hit my ball."

❖ ❖ ❖ GOVERNMENT

Govern a great nation as you would cook a small fish. Do not overdo it.

LAO-TZU

CORRESPONDENT Hedrick Smith tells this story to illustrate the uncertainties of life in the former Soviet Union: Two Russians were walking along the edge of a steep cliff one night when one slipped and fell over.

His companion crept to the edge. "Are you all right?" he shouted.

"Yes," came the answer from below.

"Are you hurt?" he shouted back down. "No," came the reply. "Well," shouted the surprised man from above, "how far did you fall?" "I don't know," came the voice from below. "I haven't hit bottom yet."

Poor government comes about when good citizens sit on their hands instead of standing on their feet.

ROBERT BAKER

THE DIFFERENCE between local government and Washington is very simple. President Ronald Reagan once pointed this out with this story about a little town:

The town had traffic signs that were only five feet high, and officials decided to raise them to seven feet, to make them easier for motorists to see. Then the federal government came in and said they had a program that would achieve the same result. They broke up all the roads in town and lowered them by two feet.

THOMAS JEFFERSON and George Washington were discussing the pros and cons of the unicameral and bicameral systems of legislation.

Jefferson favored the unicameral system, where there would be a single legislative body. Washington was for the bicameral system, or two legislative chambers. The discussion went on for some time when Washington suggested they have a cup of tea.

As they chatted, Washington suddenly turned to Jefferson and said, "You, sir, have just demonstrated the superiority of the bicameral system, by your own hand."

"How is that?" said Jefferson.

"You have poured your tea from your cup into the saucer to cool. We want the bicameral system to cool things. A measure originates in one house, and in heat is passed. The other house will serve as a wonderful cooler, and by the time the measure is debated and modified by various amendments there, it is much more likely to become an equitable law. No, we can't get along without the saucer in our system."

The chief defect of a democracy is that the only political party that knows how to run the country is always the one that's out of office.

CLIQUES of people clamoring for some special interest or self-serving project bring to mind the story of the man who decided he could make a fortune providing frog legs to restaurants.

"Judging by their noise, there are millions of frogs in this marsh near me," he told a wholesale food distributor, and he made arrangements to ship 500 frogs a month.

Two weeks went by and the entrepreneur had only a few dozen frogs. It turned out that the frogs were just like some special interest groups. They made a lot of noise, but the noise wasn't in proportion to their numbers.

A GROUP OF LAWYERS once visited Washington and called on Supreme Court Justice Louis D. Brandeis. Brandeis asked them the reason for their visit. The leader of the group said, "To see the government *in action*."

"Is that one word or two?" asked Justice Brandeis.

You may reason, speculate, complain, form mobs, spend your life railing at Congress and your rulers, but unless you import less than you export, unless you spend less than you earn, you will be eternally poor.

NOAH WEBSTER
1786

It's getting more and more difficult to support the government in the style to which it has become accustomed.

SOMEBODY once asked Confucius what the ingredients were for good government. "Sufficient food, sufficient weapons, and the confidence of the common people," he replied.

Suppose he had to eliminate one of the three, the man asked Confucius, which one would he drop?

"Weapons," said Confucius.

83

What if he had to eliminate one of the remaining two?

Confucius replied that he would eliminate food, pointing out that down through the ages hunger has always been the lot of many people. The last thing he would eliminate, Confucius said, was the confidence of the common people. "People who no longer trust their leaders are lost indeed," he said.

Democracy is measured not by its leaders doing extraordinary things, but by its citizens doing ordinary things extraordinarily well.

JOHN GARDNER

GRATITUDE ❖ ❖ ❖

MANY YEARS AGO two boys were working their way through Stanford University. Their funds got desperately low, and the idea came to them to engage Ignacy Paderewski for a piano recital. They would use the funds to help pay their board and tuition.

The great pianist's manager asked for a guarantee of $2,000. The guarantee was a lot of money in those days, but the boys agreed and proceeded to promote the concert. They worked hard, only to find that they had grossed only $1,600.

After the concert the two boys told the great artist the bad news. They gave him the entire $1,600, along with a promissory note for $400, explaining that they would earn the amount at the earliest possible moment and send the money to him. It looked like the end of their college careers.

"No, boys," replied Paderewski, "that won't do." Then, tearing the note in two, he returned the money to them as well. "Now," he told them, "take out of this $1,600 all of your expenses, and keep for each of you 10 percent of the balance for your work. Let me have the rest."

The years rolled by—World War I came and went. Paderewski, now premier of Poland, was striving to feed thousands of starving people in his native land. The only person in the world who could help him was Herbert Hoover, who was in charge of the U.S. Food and Relief Bureau. Hoover responded and soon thousands of tons of food were sent to Poland.

After the starving people were fed, Paderewski journeyed to Paris to thank Hoover for the relief sent him.

"That's all right, Mr. Paderewski," was Hoover's reply. "Besides, you don't remember it, but you helped me once when I was a student at college, and I was in trouble."

❖ ❖ ❖ **GREED**

LEO TOLSTOY once wrote a story about a successful peasant farmer who was not satisfied with his lot. He wanted more of everything.

One day he received a novel offer. For 1,000 rubles, he could buy all the land he could walk around in a day. The only condition was that he had to be back at his starting point by sundown.

Early the next morning he started out walking at a fast pace. By midday he was very tired, but he kept going, covering more and more ground. Well into the afternoon he realized that his greed had taken him far from the starting point. He quickened his pace and as the sun began to sink low in the sky, he began to run, knowing that if he did not make it back by sundown the opportunity to become an even bigger landholder would be lost.

As the sun began to sink below the horizon he came within sight of the finish line. Gasping for breath, his heart pounding, he called upon every bit of strength left in his body and staggered

85

across the line just before the sun disappeared. He immediately collapsed, blood streaming from his mouth. In a few minutes he was dead.

Afterward, his servants dug a grave. It was not much over six feet long and three feet wide.

The title of Tolstoy's story was: *How Much Land Does a Man Need?*

HAPPINESS ❖ ❖ ❖

ROBERT LOUIS STEVENSON suffered poor health from childhood until he died at age 44. But he never allowed illness to conquer his spirit. He felt that being happy was a duty and he faithfully followed a number of precepts to keep himself as happy as possible. Here they are:

Make up your mind to be happy. Learn to find pleasure in simple things.

Make the best of your circumstances. No one has everything, and everyone has some sorrow mixed in with the gladness of life. The trick is to make the laughter outweigh the tears.

Don't take yourself too seriously. Don't think that somehow you should be protected from misfortunes that befall other people.

Don't let criticism worry you. You can't please everybody.

Don't let others set your standards. Be yourself.

Do the things you enjoy doing, but don't go into debt in the process.

Don't borrow trouble. Imaginary things are harder to bear than the actual ones.

Do not cherish enmities. Don't hold grudges. Hatred poisons the soul.

Have many interests. If you can't travel, read about many places.

Don't spend your life brooding over sorrows or mistakes. Don't be one who never gets over things.

Do what you can for those less fortunate than yourself.

Keep busy at something. A very busy person never has time to be unhappy.

Happiness makes up in height for what it lacks in length.

ROBERT FROST

IF YOU WERE to go around asking people what would make them happier, you'd get answers like a new car, a bigger house, a raise in pay, winning a lottery, a face-lift, more kids, fewer kids, a new restaurant to go to—probably not one in a 100 would say *a chance to help people*. And yet that might bring the most happiness of all.

I don't know Dr. Jonas Salk, but after what he's done for us with his polio vaccine, if he isn't happy, he should have his brilliant head examined. Of course, not all of us can do what he did. I know I can't do what he did. He beat me to it.

The point is, it doesn't have to be anything that extraordinary. It can be working for a worthy cause, performing a needed service, or just doing something that helps another person.

GEORGE BURNS

We really need only five things on this earth. Some food, some sun, some work, some fun, and someone.

You can multiply happiness by dividing it.

The secret of happiness is not in doing what one likes to do, but in liking what one has to do.

SIR JAMES M. BARRIE

THERE should be no *whens* or *ifs* about the pleasure in our lives.

We should not be saying *When I win the state lottery* or *When I hit the jackpot in Las Vegas or Atlantic City.*

We should not be counting on *ifs*—*If I get that promotion,* or *If I'm lucky.* You can't count on these things.

There's plenty of pleasure in the here and now. Somebody once said that happiness is like a butterfly. Chase it, and you'll never catch it; stand still where you are, and it will light on your shoulder.

Even when they find it, some people can't live with happiness. After a great success, instead of relaxing, they develop anxieties. They worry about lawsuits, accidents, the Internal Revenue Service, and other things. They keep looking for failure.

Look for pleasure, not pain. Find pleasure in little things: friends, good food, sunshine, flowers, laughter, and service to others. Learn that happiness is, for the most part, internal. It's a gift you give to yourself, not just at birthdays or anniversaries, but all year round.

Spread happiness where you go, not when.

✦ ✦ ✦ HEALTH/HEALTH CARE

If you want to keep fit, take the advice of Adelle Davis: Eat break-fast like a king, lunch like a prince, and dinner like a pauper.

WILLIAM LINK, executive vice president of The Prudential Insurance Company, uses an old story that, he says, pretty well describes why our health-care costs are out of control.

A patient went to see a highly respected doctor for an examination. After three days of intensive tests, the patient got the bill. He rushed back to doctor's office and said, "What are you crazy, Doc? I can't pay this. Two thousand dollars! My goodness."

The doctor said, "All right, in your case, just give me half."

"Half? I can't even pay half."

"Well what portion of the bill do you think you can pay?"

"Not a penny. I'm a poor man."

"With all due respect," sighed the doctor, "why did you come to me? I don't want to be immodest, but you force me to point out that I am regarded as one of the finest specialists around."

"Listen Doc," the man replied, "when it comes to my health, money is no object."

THE LATE E.B. WHITE once discovered that the medical profession was interested in turtle blood because turtles don't suffer from arteriosclerosis in old age. The doctors wondered whether there was some special property of turtle blood that prevents the arteries from hardening.

White sat down at his typewriter and recorded *his* views on the matter.

"There is the possibility that a turtle's blood vessels stay in nice shape," he wrote, "because of the way turtles conduct their lives. Turtles rarely pass up the chance to relax in the sun on a partly submerged log. No two turtles ever lunched together with the idea of promoting anything. Turtles never use the word *implementation* or the phrases *hard core* and *in the last analysis*. No turtle ever rang another turtle back on the phone. In the last analysis, a turtle, although lacking know-how, knows how to live. A turtle, by its admirable habits, gets to the hard core of life. That may be why its arteries are so soft."

White had one afterthought: "It is worth noting," he wrote, "that Chinese do not appear to suffer arteriosclerosis nearly as much as do Occidentals, and Chinese are heavy eaters of terrapin. Maybe the answer is a double-barreled one. We should all spend more time on a log in the sun and should eat more turtle soup."

DR. KARL MENNINGER, the famous psychiatrist, once gave a lecture on mental health and was answering questions from the audience.

"What would you advise a person to do," asked one man, "if that person felt a nervous breakdown coming on?"

Most people expected him to reply: "Consult a psychiatrist." To their astonishment, he replied: "Lock up your house, go across the railway tracks, find someone in need, and do something to help that person."

❖ ❖ ❖ **HONESTY**

A CLOTHING STORE in a midwestern city set aside 200 umbrellas for the use of pedestrians on rainy days. Any person could walk in and ask for one without leaving a deposit. He or she simply left a name and address.

At the end of eight months a count showed: umbrellas on hand, 197; storm casualties, one; stolen by the public, two; new accounts opened, many.

ONE OF OUR FAVORITE baseball stories involves kids just starting to play the game. It appeared a few years ago in *Sports Illustrated* magazine.

The game was played in Wellington, Florida. In it, a seven-year-old first baseman, Tanner Munsey, fielded a ground ball and tried to tag a runner going from first to second base.

The umpire, Laura Benson, called the runner out, but young Tanner immediately ran to her side and said, "Ma'am, I didn't tag the runner." Umpire Benson reversed herself, sent the runner to second base, and Tanner's coach gave him the game ball for his honesty.

Two weeks later, Laura Benson was again the umpire and Tanner was playing shortstop when a similar play occurred. This time Benson ruled that Tanner had missed the tag on a runner going to third base, and she called the runner safe. Tanner looked at Benson and, without saying a word, tossed the ball to the catcher and returned to his position. Benson sensed something was wrong. "Did you tag the runner?" she asked Tanner.

His reply: "Yes."

Benson then called the runner out. The opposing coaches

protested until she explained what had happened two weeks earlier. "If a kid is that honest," she said, "I have to give it to him."

A SMALL BOY at summer camp received a large package of cookies in the mail from his mother. He ate a few, then placed the remainder under his bed. The next day, after lunch, he went to his tent to get a cookie. The box was gone.

That afternoon a camp counselor, who had been told of the theft, saw another boy sitting behind a tree eating the stolen cookies. "That young man," he said to himself, "must be taught not to steal."

He returned to the group and sought out the boy whose cookies had been stolen. "Billy," he said, "I know who stole your cookies. Will you help me teach him a lesson?"

"Well, yes—but aren't you going to punish him?" asked the puzzled boy.

"No, that would only make him resent and hate you," the counselor explained. "I want you to call your mother and ask her to send you another box of cookies."

The boy did as the counselor asked and a few days later received another box of cookies in the mail.

"Now," said the counselor, "the boy who stole your cookies is down by the lake. Go down there and share your cookies with him."

"But," protested the boy, "he's the thief."

"I know. But try it—see what happens."

Half an hour later the camp counselor saw the two come up the hill, arm in arm. The boy who had stolen the cookies was earnestly trying to get the other to accept his jackknife in payment for the stolen cookies, and the victim was just as earnestly refusing the gift from his new friend, saying that a few old cookies weren't that important anyway.

❖ ❖ ❖ HOPE

I KNOW THE WORLD is filled with troubles and many injustices. But reality is as beautiful as it is ugly. I think it is just as important to sing about beautiful mornings as it is to talk about slums. I just couldn't write anything without hope in it.

OSCAR HAMMERSTEIN

Of all the forces that make for a better world, none is so indispensable, none so powerful, as hope. Without hope people are only half alive. With hope they dream and think and work.

CHARLES SAWYER

Have old memories but young hopes.

Hope is the feeling that you have that the feeling you have isn't permanent.

JEAN KERR

THE SCHOOL SYSTEM in a large city had a program to help children keep up their school work during stays in the city's hospitals. One day a teacher assigned to the program received a routine call asking her to visit a particular child. She took the child's name and room number and talked briefly with the child's regular class teacher.

"We're studying nouns and adverbs in his class now," the regular teacher said, "and I'd be grateful if you could help him understand them so he doesn't fall too far behind."

The hospital program teacher went to see the boy that afternoon. No one had mentioned to her that the boy had been badly burned and was in great pain. Upset at the sight of the boy, she stammered as she told him, "I've been sent by your school to help you with nouns and adverbs." When she left she felt she hadn't accomplished much.

But the next day, a nurse asked her, "What did you do to that boy?" The teacher felt she must have done something wrong and began to apologize.

"No, no," said the nurse. "You don't know what I mean. We've been worried about that little boy, but ever since yesterday, his whole attitude has changed. He's fighting back, responding to treatment. It's as though he's decided to live."

Two weeks later the boy explained that he had completely given up hope until the teacher arrived. Everything changed when he came to a simple realization. He expressed it this way: "They wouldn't send a teacher to work on nouns and adverbs with a dying boy, would they?"

HUMILITY ❖ ❖ ❖

NO GREATER CHANGE of environment for the U.S. Supreme Court could have been imagined when that august body moved from its dingy, smelly basement room in the Capitol Building to its present location—an awesome, sumptuous $11-million marble temple of justice. At least one of the justices was a bit unhappy over the change—Justice Louis D. Brandeis.

"I would much prefer to have the Court use the little room," the troubled jurist confided to a friend.

"You would?" the other rejoined. "Why?"

"Because," replied Justice Brandeis, "our little room kept us humble."

———————

BENJAMIN FRANKLIN was a cocky young man. He had supreme self-confidence and believed that no one who ever lived knew more or could do more than he.

But fortunately for him, at some point in his youth he sensed that something was wrong. Things were not working out the way he had expected they would. Not all his projects were successful. Not all he said, even when true, was believed.

At that point, he showed some intelligence. He backed away and took a long, hard look at himself, with the result that he completely reformed. Now in place of cocksure statements, he expressed himself in terms of utter humility. Now in place of blurting out his opinions, he deftly asked the other persons for theirs. Now instead of being dogmatic he became exceedingly humble.

And that change of tack worked so well that it was not long before this youngster was the most successful man in his city, Philadelphia. And to this day anyone who wants to explain the true course of success in the world, real success, success in many endeavors, cannot find a better example than Mr. Franklin.

During his long life, once he had reoriented himself and started trying to please others, Benjamin Franklin was never again at loggerheads with anyone. Wherever he went, he was revered; whomever he met, he charmed; whatever he wanted for himself or for his country, he got.

It is a great lesson in humility which you can learn from this man; a lesson that can have only one result—vastly improved human relations, and more success in all your dealings with the world.

IDEAS ❖ ❖ ❖

A new idea is delicate. It can be killed by a sneer or a yawn; it can be stabbed to death by a quip, and worried to death by a frown on the right man's brow.

CHARLIE BROWER

Great ideas need landing gear as well as wings.

PRESENTING an idea and convincing people of its value is a lot like courtship. Easy does it. To avoid resistance, use an oblique rather than a head-to-head approach. "Have you thought about this?" is a much better way to reveal your idea rather than a flat "This is the way it should be." The latter approach is likely to create antagonism. The former gets people thinking about your idea. Next thing you know, some people may be arguing for your case, not against it.

Presenting your own objections or misgivings often helps. "The best way to convince another," Benjamin Franklin said, "is to state your case moderately and accurately. Then say of course you may be mistaken about it; which causes your listener to receive what you have to say and, like as not, turn about and convince you of it, since you are in doubt."

The person with a new idea is a crank until the idea succeeds.

MARK TWAIN

❖ ❖ ❖ IMAGINATION

ONE of the most dramatic stories to come out of the Vietnam War was that of Air Force Colonel George Hall.

While in solitary confinement, he played an imaginary round of golf each day for five and one-half years as a prisoner of war in North Vietnam. In his black pajamas and bare feet and in his solitary cube, he would put a golf ball down and hit his drives, straight and true, down the middle of a plush green fairway, perhaps Pebble Beach or Augusta National. Every course he had played before, he replayed in his imagination for five and one-half years. He replaced every divot, chipped onto the green, blasted balls out of sand traps, then raked the traps smooth again, pulled out the flag, got on one knee and checked the break to see whether the ball would break toward the ocean or down the slope, putted down the hole, and walked on to the next tee, washing his ball in the ball wash of his imagination.

Colonel Hall recognized that we have two choices in life: Either play back haunting thoughts of fears, disease, death, and hopelessness, or play back winning experiences from the past and previews of winning performances to come.

Those mental stimulations paid off when he was finally released and got back to the real things. After all those years in solitary confinement and less than a month after his release, he was back in form.

Colonel Hall played in the New Orleans Open, paired with Orville Moody, the old pro. The colonel shot a 76!

When it was over, a reporter congratulated him and said, "That was really what you call beginner's reentry luck, right?"

Colonel Hall smiled and said, "Not really. I never three-putted a green in all my five and one-half years."

DENIS WAITLEY in
The Winner's Edge
Berkley Books

97

WHEN TEMPERATURES SOAR many people enjoy iced tea. The next time *you* do, remember Richard Blechnyden.

Blechnyden was a man who went to the St. Louis World's Fair in 1904 to promote teas from India and Ceylon. Up to that time tea had been drunk hot, but the temperatures during the fair were in the high 90s and no one was interested in sampling Mr. Blechnyden's tea. Then it dawned on him that iced drink stands were doing a tremendous business.

He decided to make his tea an iced drink too. He made it stronger than usual to compensate for the diluting effect of the ice, added some sugar, and he was in business. People loved it, and now they drink it all over the world.

Pass the lemon, please, and let us drink to Richard Blechnyden.

INDISPENSABILITY ❖ ❖ ❖

Sometime when you feel that your going
Would leave an unfillable hole,
Just follow these simple instructions
And see how they humble your soul.

Take a bucket and fill it with water,
Put your hand in it up to your wrist,
Pull it out and the hole that's remaining
Is a measure of how you'll be missed.

You can splash all you wish when you enter,
You may stir up the water galore,
But stop, and you'll find that in no time
It looks quite the same as before.

WALTER DAMROSCH became a full-fledged conductor when he was still in his 20s. Not unexpectedly, the acclaim he received went to his head. He began to think that no one could take his place. Then one day at rehearsal he misplaced his baton.

"Is there an extra baton around?" he asked.

Three violinists immediately produced batons from their inside coat pockets. Sobered by this, Damrosch never again regarded himself as indispensable.

❖ ❖ ❖ INGENUITY

HERE'S an old idea that could be useful in today's environmentally conscious world.

Back in the 1800s, China used to ship fragile pottery to Europe packed in tea leaves inside carved wooden crates. The tea leaves were ideal as packaging material, and the European shop owners found that their pottery always arrived intact. The shop owners would sell the pottery, sell the crates as end tables or decorator objects, and grind up the leaves and sell them as tea. Nothing was wasted.

DID YOU ever see the report issued by the Club of Rome in 1971? This group of experts studied the problem of economic growth. With the aid of computers, the study predicted that growth would be limited by the depletion of nonrenewable sources of energy (coal, oil, and natural gas) and by the accumulation of pollution.

The remedy they proposed was a drastic one—stop growing. Among other things, the Club of Rome predicted that we would be running out of copper about now. They reached that conclusion by taking the rate of copper consumption 20 years ago and increasing the consumption by the expected rate of economic

99

growth. They could not know that by 1991 we would be replacing copper telephone wires with glass fibers. These fibers are made from the most common element in the earth's crust and they can carry thousands of times more information than the best copper cable. What they left out of their calculation, in this prediction and others, was the ingenuity of the human race to constantly develop new resources.

THOMAS R. KOHN

Edison Electric Institute

DURING WORLD WAR I a Protestant chaplain with the American troops in Italy became a friend of a local Roman Catholic priest.

In time, the chaplain moved on with his unit and was killed. The priest heard of his death and asked military authorities if the chaplain could be buried in the cemetery behind his church. Permission was granted.

But the priest ran into a problem with his own Catholic Church authorities. They were sympathetic, but they said they could not approve of the burial of a non-Catholic in a Catholic cemetery. So the priest buried his friend just outside the cemetery fence.

Years later, a war veteran who knew what had happened returned to Italy and visited the old priest. The first thing he did was ask to see the chaplain's grave. To his surprise, he found the grave inside the fence.

"Ah," he said, "I see you got permission to move the body."

"No," said the priest. "They told me where I couldn't bury the body. But nobody told me I couldn't move the fence."

❖ ❖ ❖   INVENTIONS

EARLY IN HIS CAREER, Thomas Edison invented a vote-recording machine for use in legislative chambers. By moving a switch to the right or left, an official could vote for or against a proposal without leaving his desk. The machine would replace the tedious business of marking and counting ballots.

Elated with the prospects, Edison obtained a patent—his first—and headed for Washington. Eagerly he demonstrated his machine to the chairman of Congressional Committees. This gentleman, while complimenting Edison on his ingenuity, promptly turned it down. "Filibustering and delay in the tabulation of votes are often the only means we have for defeating bad or improper legislation," he told Edison.

The young inventor was stunned. The invention was good; he knew it and the chairman knew it. Still, it wasn't wanted. Said Edison later: "There and then I made a vow that I would never again invent anything which was not wanted."

It's a good thing for all of us to remember. No rule for success is more fundamental than giving the boss—or the customer—what they really want, not what we think they *ought* to want.

MARK TWAIN was fascinated by inventions. In his lifetime he lost more than half a million dollars investing in various contraptions.

Once, after a series of bad investments had temporarily tempered his enthusiasm for new gadgets, he was approached by a tall young man with a mysterious device under his arm.

The young man was looking for some financial backing to develop and market his device. Twain listened politely to what the

101

young man had to say, but explained that he had been burned once too often and was not interested.

"But I'm not asking you to invest a fortune," the young man said. "You can have a large share in this for $500."

The author shook his head and the young man sadly walked away. Twain felt a twinge of regret—not enough to change his mind, but enough to call after the poor fellow, "What did you say your name was again?"

"Bell," was the reply. "Alexander Graham Bell."

JUSTICE ❖ ❖ ❖

As MAYOR of New York City, Fiorello La Guardia liked to keep in touch with all the various departments under him. Often he would fill in for the department heads or officeholders as a way of accomplishing this.

One time he chose to preside over Night Court. It was a cold winter night and a trembling man was brought before him charged with stealing a loaf of bread. His family, he said, was starving.

"I have to punish you," declared La Guardia. "There can be no exceptions to the law. I fine you $10." As he said this, however, The Little Flower was reaching into his own pocket for the money. He tossed the bill into his famous sombrero. "Here's the $10 to pay your fine—which I now remit," he said.

"Furthermore," he declared, "I'm going to fine everybody in this courtroom 50 cents for living in a city where a man has to steal bread in order to eat. Mr. Bailiff, collect the fines and give them to the defendant!"

The hat was passed and the incredulous man, with a smile on his face, left the courtroom with a stake of $47.50.

❖ ❖ ❖ KINDNESS

A word of kindness is seldom spoken in vain. It is treasured by the recipient for life. Clever sayings are as easily lost as pearls slipping from a broken string.

IT TAKES MANY HOURS to fill a pail of water if you're doing it drop by drop. Even when the pail seems full, it can take many drops more. Eventually, of course, one drop more makes the pail overflow.

So it is with kindness. Most people appreciate even one deed of kindness, but some find it difficult to show their appreciation. Don't let this stop you. Eventually you'll do some little thing that will make their hearts overflow.

MARY, a woman in her late thirties, was driving home one night with her two small children. It was 10:30 on a rainy, drizzly evening.

As Mary reached her neighborhood, she turned off the main highway and went through an underpass. Suddenly, on the side of the road she saw an old car jacked up, obviously in trouble. A man was working on it. Sitting on the curbstone in the drizzle was a woman with a baby in her arms and a small child beside her.

Mary stopped her car and got out to see whether she could help. Help, they said, was on the way—the man had phoned his brother. Nonetheless, Mary insisted that the woman, the baby, and the child join her and her two children in her car. She kept them warm, dry, and in good spirits for two hours—until the brother arrived.

A week later there was a knock on Mary's door. When she opened it, there was the woman, carrying a bouquet of paper flowers she had made especially for Mary.

Fifteen years later—there was another knock on Mary's door. It was the same woman. "We were passing through the neighborhood," she said, "and wondered whether you still lived here. There's something I've always wanted to tell you. We come from Puerto Rico, you see, and when people from Puerto Rico get together they often tell each other stories about how mean some Americans have been to them. Whenever I hear a story like that, I tell them about you. I thought you'd like to know."

"What is good?"
I asked in musing mood.
Order, said the law court;
Knowledge, said the school;
Truth, said the wise man;
Pleasure, said the fool;
Love, said the maiden;
Beauty, said the page;
Freedom, said the dreamer;
Home, said the sage;
Fame, said the soldier;
Equity, the seer;
Spoke my heart full sadly:
"The answer is not here."
Then within my bosom
Softly this I heard:
"Each heart holds the secret;
Kindness is the word."

JOHN BOYLE O'REILLY

You cannot do a kindness too soon, because you never know how soon it will be too late.

WHO AMONG US has not been thrilled by Beethoven's *Moonlight Sonata?*

It captures in sound the glory of a moonlit night—glory that is difficult to describe in words. This beautiful piece of music came to be because Beethoven wanted to give something of himself and his talent to a blind girl. He put his genius to work to produce in sound the beauty that her eyes could not behold. He gave the best of his talent in a selfless act of kindness. As a result, the world has been enriched.

No one is useless in this world who lightens the burden of another.

CHARLES DICKENS

WHEN YOU THINK of a nice thing to do for someone, don't just think it. Do it.

When you have a kind thought, express it. Bring it to life. Put it into action.

If you admire something someone has said or done, speak up and say so. You will both be the richer for it.

Never be content to *think* nice thoughts. *Express* them, and *do* them.

❖ ❖ ❖ **LAUGHTER**

A BOOK issued by the Army years ago gave all manner of advice to noncommissioned officers. It even tells how to make men who have quarreled friends again. The men are put to washing the same window, one outside, the other inside.

Looking at each other, they soon have to laugh and all is forgotten. It works: I have tried it.

LUDWIG BEMELMANS

CHI CHI RODRIGUEZ was voted into the Golf Hall of Fame in 1992 and Jerry Izenberg, the sports columnist for the *Newark* (NJ) *Star-Ledger*, interviewed him to mark the occasion. Jerry's story contained a message that bears repeating.

When Chi Chi was five, his parents were waiting for him to die. He had what was called sprue.

Chi Chi remembers his mother, Modesta, kneeling on the floor to pray for him, which was about all she could do. For two years, with a lot of prayer and sporadic medical help, he survived. Then a doctor tested him at the medical clinic and told his parents that there was only three or four months of life left in Chi Chi's little body. But Chi Chi didn't die.

Other troubles began to plague the family. His father, who had worked 15 hours a day on one of the nearby ranches, had a heart attack. He lost his job and couldn't get another. Hunger was always a problem.

But Chi Chi kept surviving. Before long he got a job caddying and learned to play golf. What followed was a successful career on the professional golf tour and an even more successful one on the senior tour. Now he's in the Hall of Fame.

The fact that he has always given unstintingly of his time, his money, and himself to help poor and disadvantaged kids made him a popular figure in the sports world and no doubt helped him when the Hall of Fame votes were cast.

It's been a long, hard road, but to this day he gives a major share of credit to one thing that helped him all along the way—his ability to laugh.

"When they (critics) say I laugh too much just to get attention on the course, it depresses me," Rodriguez told Jerry Izenberg. "There could be 20,000 people on a golf course at a big tournament and if there are, then I want to make 20,000 friends on that day. You owe them something."

"You owe them a lot more than just a smile," said Chi Chi. "Look around this room," he said, gesturing out over a plush hotel restaurant. "Who laughs? I mean, who really laughs? Most people don't. They just worry about yesterdays. Man, I had my yesterdays! That's not what living is all about."

Build for yourself a strongbox,
  Fashion each part with care;
When it's strong as your hand can make it,
  Put all your troubles there;
Hide there all thoughts of your failures,
  And each bitter cup that you quaff;
Lock all your heartaches within it,
  Then sit on the lid and laugh.
Tell no one its contents,
  Never its secrets share;
When you've dropped in your care and worry
  Keep them forever there;
Hide them from sight so completely
  That the world will never dream half;
Fasten the strongbox securely—
  Then sit on the lid and laugh.

BERTHA ADAMS BACKUS

LEADERSHIP ❖ ❖ ❖

ALEXANDER THE GREAT once led his forces across a scorching terrain. For 11 days they pressed on and the survivors were weary, their throats parched.

One day, those in his advance guard brought Alexander a helmet containing a cup or two of water that they had been able to find. The troops watched with envy as the water was presented to him.

Alexander never hesitated. He dumped the water on the hot sand at his feet and said, "It's no use for one to drink when many thirst." His troops desperately needed water, but what he had in his helmet represented only a drop or two for each individual. He didn't have the quantity of water they needed, but he gave them something else—inspiration. They found water later, but at that moment, he gave them something that was more important—leadership.

PRESIDENT HARRY S TRUMAN visited Mexico in 1947 despite considerable concern in Washington about anti-American feelings among Mexicans.

While there, he made an unexpected appearance at Chapultepec Castle, the West Point of Mexico. A hundred years earlier, General Winfield Scott's troops had stormed the heights and captured the castle in the war between the United States and Mexico. The only survivors were six cadets who committed suicide rather than surrender.

Years later, Merle Miller asked about the Chapultepec visit while interviewing Truman for his biography, *Plain Speaking* (Berkley).

"When I first suggested it," said the President, "everybody, *everybody* said I couldn't do it. They trotted out all the so-called protocol experts, and they all said no. Those birds, all they know how to say is, 'You can't do this and you can't do that.' And if you ask them *why* you can't, all it ever adds up to is, 'It's never been done before.' They went on to say that if I did it, it would remind the Mexicans of the war with the United States, and they'd resent that. And some others said that if I paid tribute to those Mexican boys, it was going to alienate the Texans."

There is a monument to *Los Niños Heroes* at Chapultepec and, despite the misgivings of the protocol people, Truman went there, placed a wreath on it, and bowed his head in tribute. The cadets in the Mexican color guard burst into tears. It was said that in the history of the two countries, nothing has ever been done that was so helpful in cementing their relationship.

NAPOLEON'S GENIUS has been attributed to many things, but above all, he was a superb leader. Like any wise leader he was aware that his own success would have been nothing had his men not been willing, even eager, to follow him. Obviously he could not know and personally inspire every man in his vast army; therefore he devised a simple technique for circumventing this difficulty. Before visiting a regiment he would call the colonel aside and ask for the name of a soldier who had served well in previous campaigns, but who had not been given the credit he deserved.

The colonel would indicate such a man. Napoleon would then learn everything about him, where he was born, the names of his family, his exploits in battle, etc.

Later, upon passing this man while reviewing the troops, and at a signal from the colonel, Napoleon would stop, single out the man, greet him warmly, ask about his family, compliment him on his bravery and loyalty, reminisce about old campaigns, then pin a medal on the grateful soldier.

The gesture worked. After the review, the other soldiers

would remark, "You see, he knows us—he remembers. He knows our families. He knows we have served."

General Eisenhower used to demonstrate the art of leadership with a simple piece of string. He'd put it on a table and say: Pull it and it'll follow wherever you wish. Push it and it will go nowhere at all. It's just that way when it comes to leading people.

THE DAY WAS COLD AND BLEAK. George Washington, starting out from his headquarters, drew on his greatcoat, turned up the collar, and pulled his hat down to shield his face from the biting wind. As he walked down the road to where the soldiers were fortifying a camp, no one would have known that the tall, muffled figure was the Commander-in-Chief of the Army.

As he came near the camp he stopped to watch a small company of soldiers, under the command of a corporal, building a breastwork of logs. The men were tugging at a heavy log. The corporal, important and superior, stood at one side giving orders.

"Up with it!" he cried. "Now all together! Push. Up with it, I say!" The men gathered new strength. A great push and the log was nearly in its place, but it was too heavy. Just before it reached the top of the pile it slipped and fell back.

The corporal shouted again. "Up with it! What ails you? Up with it!" The men tugged and strained again. The log nearly reached the top, slipped, and once more rolled back.

"Heave hard!" cried the corporal. "One, two, three—now push!"

Another struggle and then, just as the log was about to roll back for the third time, Washington ran forward, pushed with all his strength, and the log rolled into place on top of the breastwork. The men, panting and perspiring, sought to thank him, but he turned toward the corporal. "Why don't you help your men with this heavy lifting, when they need another hand?" he asked.

"Why don't I?" asked the man. "Don't you see I am a corporal?"

"Indeed," replied Washington, throwing open his greatcoat and showing his uniform. "I am only the Commander-in-Chief. Next time you have a log too heavy for your men to lift, send for me!"

SUPERIOR LEADERS get things done with very little motion. They impart instruction not through many words, but through a few deeds. They keep informed about everything but interfere hardly at all. They are catalysts, and though things would not get done as well if they weren't there, when they succeed they take no credit. And because they take no credit, credit never leaves them.

LAO-TZU

THE ABILITY to make people like you is one of the most valuable talents you can possibly possess. Without it, your other talents—no matter how great—may be largely wasted. You may never get a chance to use them in a way that would do the greatest good, for yourself or for others.

Strong statements? Yes—but they happen to be true. Anyone in a leadership role, whether it be chief executive officer or supervisor of a small workforce, can't afford to ignore them.

Likability is one of the fundamental ingredients of good leadership. People are more willing to follow someone they like than someone they don't. Being likable is also important in making friends, winning a mate, getting and holding a job, winning

111

recognition, and getting a raise. Those who ignore it do so to their own detriment.

There are many things any boss can do to be more likable. Here are just a few:

1. *Smile!* Greet people with a smile, smile whenever you pass them, smile when you say good night. Don't be a grouch concerned only with your own feelings or importance.

2. Take a sincere interest in people and their problems. Ask questions and listen. Forget your own problems for a while.

3. Be fair to everyone, not just to a few special people you happen to like.

4. Notice what people do well and praise them for it. Also notice when people try hard, even if the results leave much to be desired. Praise them for trying. Assure them that if they keep it up, they'll soon be doing better.

5. *Never* lose your temper! Keep your cool regardless of the circumstances.

There's nothing new about these ideas. They are so vital, however, that if you learn to practice them, you might not need many others. And people would not only like you more, they'd respect you more as a result.

JOHN LUTHER

———————

DWIGHT MORROW, the father of Anne Morrow Lindbergh, once held a dinner party to which Calvin Coolidge had been invited. After Coolidge left, Morrow told the remaining guests that Coolidge would make a good president. The others disagreed. They felt Coolidge was too quiet, that he lacked color and personality. No one would like him, they said.

Anne, then age six, spoke up: "I like him," she said. Then she displayed a finger with a small bandage around it. "He was the only one at the party who asked about my sore finger."

"And that's why he would make a good president," added Morrow.

———————

NINE-YEAR-OLD GRACE BEDELL, who lived in Westfield, a small town in upstate New York, saw a picture of Abraham Lincoln shortly after he was elected President of the United States. It occurred to her that the President would look more impressive if he had whiskers so she wrote him a letter to that effect.

President Lincoln wrote back, pointing out that people might think that growing a beard was a silly affectation. Grace came right back with another letter saying it was the right thing to do because he looked too solemn.

On his way from Illinois to Washington for his inauguration, Lincoln ordered his special train to stop at Westfield, where he appeared on the rear platform and announced, "I have a correspondent in this town named Grace Bedell, and if she's present, I hope she'll step forward.

"Here I am!" cried the astonished Grace. "Well, Grace," said Lincoln, leaning over the rear rail, "I let these whiskers grow for you. I hope you think I'm looking better now."

"You look wonderful now," the little girl assured him, "and I bet you're going to be the greatest President this country ever had!"

Mr. Lincoln put his stovepipe hat on his head and the train chugged away.

———————

WHAT this country needs is more people to inspire others with confidence, and fewer people to discourage any initiative in the right direction; more to get into the thick of things, fewer to sit on the sidelines merely finding fault; more to point out what's right with the world, and fewer to keep harping on what's wrong with it; and more who are interested in lighting candles, and fewer who blow them out.

FATHER JAMES KELLER

Founder of The Christophers

LEADERS must be resourceful, cool when the unexpected occurs, able to think on their feet, and get things back on track when plans go awry. This Christmas story illustrates the point.

A little boy had aspirations to be cast as Joseph in the school Nativity play, but he lost out to a classmate. The teacher in charge gave him the minor role of the innkeeper instead, and he was bitterly disappointed. During the weeks of rehearsal, he brooded and thought only of revenge.

On the evening of the performance, Joseph and Mary came on stage and knocked on the door of the inn. The innkeeper opened the door slightly and Joseph spoke his line, "We seek board and lodging for the night." Then Joseph stepped back, awaiting the innkeeper's rebuff, "There is no room in the inn."

But the innkeeper hadn't pondered all these weeks for naught. Gleefully, he flung the door wide open and cried, "Come in. Come in! I can give you the best room in the house!"

Joseph stared at the innkeeper. Then with great presence of mind, he said to Mary, "Stay here. I'll see what the room looks like." When he reappeared, he shook his head and said, "No way am I going to take my wife into a place like that. Come on, Mary, we'll sleep in the stable."

Things were back on track.

114

❖ ❖ ❖ **LIFE/LIVING**

Our business in life is not to get ahead of others, but to get ahead of ourselves—to break our own records, to outstrip our yesterday by our today.

STEWART B. JOHNSON

BEFORE you can write a check, you must make out a deposit slip. Before you can draw money out of a bank, you must put money into the bank. Before you are entitled to a living, you must give the world a life. If you want to make a first-class living, learn to give the world a first-class life.

WILLIAM J. H. BOETCKER

Treat the light things in life very seriously, and the serious things very lightly.

ELSA MAXWELL

GREAT ART is not restricted to painting, writing, sculpture, or music. There's another art at which we all can excel. It is what Henry Thoreau called the highest of arts—the art of living.

People who practice it are not artists in the usual sense. They are people who, through the nobility of their lives, have affected what Thoreau called *the quality of the day.*

Years ago, Myles Connolly, the playwright, wrote a piece about what Thoreau was talking about. Connolly pointed out that there are countless obscure people who practice this art—good people who quietly affect the lives of those about them without

115

even being aware they are doing it, winning no commendation and expecting none.

"Everybody at one time or another has known such people, strangers, relatives, or friends," said Connolly, "who have changed the quality of the day for others. They come into a room in a dark hour—a sickroom, say, or a death room, a room without hope, or merely in an hour when we are lonely or discouraged. They may say little, if anything. But the shining quality of goodness radiates from them, from their mere presence, and where there was dark there is light, where there was cowardice there is courage, and where there was listlessness there is love of life.

"These friends and relatives—or wonderful strangers met at a picnic or a hospital waiting room—all these, humble and unaware, carry with them the kindness and generosity of their lives. These are the greatest artists," said the playwright. "They practice the highest of arts—the art of living, the art of life itself."

You can't do much about the length of your life, but you can do a lot about its depth and width.

WHAT MOST PEOPLE WANT—young or old—is not merely security, or comfort, or luxury, although they are glad enough to have these. Most of all they want *meaning* in their lives. If our era and our culture and our leaders do not, or cannot, offer great meanings, great objectives, great convictions, then people will settle for shallow and trivial substitutes. This is a deficiency for which we all bear a responsibility . . . . This is the challenge of our times.

Rockefeller Report on Education
1958

Life is like a ten-speed bike. Most of us have gears we never use.

There are two things to aim at in life: first, to get what you want; and after that to enjoy it. Only the wisest of people achieve the second.

LOGAN PEARSALL SMITH

AUTHOR/TEACHER LEO BUSCAGLIA has a soft spot in his heart for Julia Child.

"I like her attitude," he says. "I watch her because she does such wonderful things: *'Tonight we're going to make a soufflé.'* And she beats this and whisks that, and she drops things on the floor and wipes her face with her napkin. And she does all these wonderful human things. Then she takes this soufflé and throws it in the oven, and talks to you for a while. Then she says, *'Now it's ready.'* When she opens the oven up, the soufflé caves in.

"You know what she does? She doesn't kill herself. She doesn't commit hara-kiri with her butcher knife. She says, *'Well, you can't win 'em all. Bon appetit.'*

"That's the way we have to live our lives. You can't win 'em all. But I know people who are still flagellating themselves over mistakes they made 20 years ago. They say 'I should have done this' and 'I should have done that.'

"Well, it's tough that you didn't. But who knows what surprises there are in tomorrow? Learn to say *'Bon appetit.'* Life is a picnic and you can make some mistakes. Nobody said you were perfect. It might even be more interesting. You burned the dinner, so you go *out.*"

Count your life by smiles, not tears. Count your age by friends, not years.

LISTENING ❖ ❖ ❖

It's all right to hold a conversation as long as you let go of it once in a while.

"LISTENING," said Dr. Karl Menninger, "is a magnetic and strange thing, a creative force. The friends who listen to us are the ones we move toward, and we want to sit in their radius. When we are listened to, it creates us, makes us unfold and expand. I discovered this a few years ago. Before that, when I went to a party I would think anxiously: 'Now try hard, be lively.' But now I tell myself to listen with affection to anyone who talks to me. This person is showing me his soul. It is a little dry and meager and full of grinding talk just now, but soon he will begin to think. He will show his true self, will be wonderfully alive."

Nature arranges it so that we can't shut our ears but that we can shut our mouths.

LITTLE THINGS ❖ ❖ ❖

Too often we underestimate the power of a touch, a smile, a kind word, a listening ear, an honest compliment, or the smallest act of caring, all of which have the potential to turn a life around.

LEO BUSCAGLIA

It's the little things that matter most. What good is a bathtub without a plug?

Most of us will never do great things, but we can do small things in a great way.

If you do enough little things every day, big things will come to you asking to be done.

A LITTLE TOWN is where everybody knows what everybody else is doing, but they read the weekly newspaper to see who got caught at it.

In a little town everybody knows every neighbor's car by sight and most by sound. They also know when they come and where they go.

A little town is where, if you get the wrong number, you can talk for 15 minutes anyway, if you want to.

A little town is where there's hardly anything to do and never enough time to do it.

In any town, the ratio of good people to bad people is a hundred to one. In a big town, the hundred are uncomfortable. In a little town, the one is.

Small-town gossip tends to cut down anybody who's up, and help up anybody who's down.

The small-town policeman has a first name. The small-town teacher has the last word.

In the class play, there's a part for everybody.

In the town jail, there's rarely anybody.

In the town cemetery, you're still among friends.

PAUL HARVEY
Grit

LOVE ❖ ❖ ❖

We do not fall in love, we grow in love and love grows in us.

KARL MENNINGER

Loving can cost a lot, but *not* loving always costs more.

MERLE SHAIN

AN EXECUTIVE WE KNOW had to put her mother in a nursing home recently. It was a painful decision, but it brought to mind a beautiful story told by Marcia Schwartz in *Guideposts* magazine. It's about a visit to her grandmother in a nursing home:

"Nice you've come," my grandmother whispered weakly from the bed. Just the night before we had brought her to the nursing home because it now took several people to move her large-boned, crippled body. Her complexion looked pasty in the morning light and her colorless hair was wispy against her pillow. Grandma, always so active, always doing for others. Now her hands lay limp on the sheets—hands that once served heaps of potatoes and fried chicken on blue willow plates, kneaded bread, patched overalls, gathered eggs, and churned butter.

I shoved my hands into the pockets of my coat. I felt helpless and awkward, not knowing what to do or say.

Several days later, I went to a doctor for a routine treatment. My three-year-old son stood wide-mouthed with fear and concern as we waited.

"Don't worry," I reassured him. "I'm all right."

Then he took my hand and held it quietly in his two small ones. My heart flooded with warmth and thankfulness. And suddenly with my little boy holding my hand, I knew what I would do the very next time I visited my grandmother.

Love lights more fire than hate extinguishes.

ELLA WHEELER WILCOX

PEOPLE need people. Laurie was about three when one night she requested my aid in getting undressed. I was downstairs and she was upstairs, and . . . well. "You know how to undress yourself," I reminded.

"Yes," she explained, "but sometimes people need people anyway, even if they do know how to do things by themselves."

As I slowly lowered the newspaper a strong feeling came over me, a mixture of delight, embarrassment, and pride; delight in the realization that what I had just heard crystallized many stray thoughts on interpersonal behavior; anger because Laurie stated so effortlessly what I had been struggling with for months; and pride because, after all, she is my daughter.

WILLIAM C. SCHUTZ

LOYALTY ❖ ❖ ❖

YOU CAN BUY people's time; you can buy their physical presence at a given place; you can even buy a measured number of their skilled muscular motions per hour. But you cannot buy enthusiasm . . . you cannot buy loyalty . . . you cannot buy the devotion of hearts, minds, or souls. You must earn these.

CLARENCE FRANCIS

A FAMOUS SINGER once contracted to appear at a Paris opera house. Ticket sales boomed, and the night of the concert found the house full and every ticket sold.

A feeling of anticipation and excitement was in the air as the house manager stepped out on the stage and announced, "Ladies and gentlemen, thank you for your enthusiastic support, but I have news that may be disappointing to some. An accident, not serious in nature but serious enough, will prevent the man you have come to hear from performing tonight." He went on to give the name of the understudy who would step into the role, but the crowd groaned and drowned it out. The excitement in the audience turned to bitter disappointment and frustration as the opera began.

The stand-in artist gave the performance everything he had. Throughout the evening, there had been nothing but an uneasy silence. Even at the end, no one applauded.

Then from the balcony, the thin voice of a little girl broke the silence. "Daddy," she called out, "I think you were wonderful."

The crowd broke into thunderous applause.

DURING quail season in Georgia, an Atlanta journalist met an old farmer hunting with an ancient pointer at his side. Twice the dog ran rheumatically ahead and pointed. Twice his master fired into the open air. When the journalist saw no birds rise, he asked the farmer for an explanation.

"Shucks," grinned the old man, "I knew there weren't no birds in that grass. Spot's nose ain't what it used to be. But him and me have had some wonderful times together. He's still doing the best he can—and it'd be mighty mean of me to call him a liar at this stage of the game!"

❖ ❖ ❖ LUCK

I am a great believer in luck, and I find the harder I work, the more I have of it.

STEPHEN LEACOCK

LUCK is seldom the fickle lady she is often pictured as being. She is more apt to bestow her favors on the deserving than the undeserving. She is especially apt to smile on people who have developed a consuming interest in their work.

Alexander Graham Bell's wife was practically deaf. For months he worked passionately to invent a workable hearing aid for her. Just as it seemed he had failed, his work led to the discovery of the principles for the telephone.

Luck had smiled—but on a very deserving man!

You never meet that terrific person until the day before your vacation ends.

ANN L. MOORE

LUCK is always waiting for something to turn up. Labor, with keen eyes and strong will, always turns up something. Luck lies in bed and wishes the postman will bring news of a legacy. Labor turns out at six o'clock and with busy pen or ringing hammer, lays the foundation of a competence. Luck whines. Labor whistles. Luck relies on chance, labor on character.

RICHARD COBDEN

MARRIAGE ❖ ❖ ❖

To keep a fire burning brightly there's one easy rule: Keep the logs together, near enough to keep warm and far enough apart for breathing room. Good fire, good marriage, same rule.

MARNIE REED CROWEL

A YOUNG COUPLE walked into a bridal shop and asked to see a bridal gown and headpiece.

The young woman obviously loved one particular gown and the salesperson suggested that she try it on. Moments later she emerged from a dressing room and stood, a radiant figure in white, in front of her companion. He gazed at her in adoration.

"Do you think you would like to take it?" the salesperson asked.

124

"Oh, I wish I could, but we can't afford it," said the woman. "I just wanted my husband to see me dressed the way I might have been. We were married a half hour ago."

A good marriage is the union of two forgivers.

RUTH BELL GRAHAM

One advantage of marriage, it seems to me, is that when you fall out of love with him, or he falls out of love with you, it keeps you together until you maybe fall *in* again.

JUDITH VIORST

✦ ✦ ✦ MILITARY

THE LATE General Emmet "Rosey" O'Donnell used to tell this story about an incident early in his career. He was a lieutenant at a U.S. Air Force base near Denver, Colorado, when the commanding general of the base ordered O'Donnell to do something. Lt. O'Donnell, with what could be called foolish courage, suggested a better way.

"O'Donnell," said the commanding officer, "are you proposing to countermand an order?"

"General, sir," replied O'Donnell, "I'm sure you didn't reach your present rank by being a *yes* man."

"No," said the general, "but that's how I made colonel."

MISTAKES ❖ ❖ ❖

The biggest mistake you can make is to believe that you are working for someone else.

Learn from the mistakes of others—you can never live long enough to make them all yourself.

THE ROMAN philosopher and statesman, Cicero, wrote this some 2000 years ago:

The Six Mistakes of Man

1. The delusion that personal gain is made by crushing others.

2. The tendency to worry about things that cannot be changed or corrected.

3. Insisting that a thing is impossible because we cannot accomplish it.

4. Refusing to set aside trivial preferences.

5. Neglecting development and refinement of the mind, and not acquiring the habit of reading and studying.

6. Attempting to compel others to believe and live as we do.

A HUSKY FELLOW entered a bar and said, "The sign in your window says you're looking for a bouncer. Is the job filled?"

"Nope," said the bartender, "how much experience have you had?"

"Some," said the burly fellow, "but let me show you what I can do. Watch this." He walked down to the end of the bar, where a loud-mouthed man was holding forth. He lifted the man off his bar stool, took him to the door, and threw him out into the street.

Returning to the bartender, the big fellow said, "How's that?"

"Just fine," said the bartender. "But you'll have to ask the boss about the job. I only work here."

"Okay," said the big guy. "Where is he?"

"Just coming back in the front door."

IN A SMALL PUB in the highlands of Scotland a group of fishermen gathered one afternoon and were enjoying a round of ale. Just as one was showing, with his hands, how big one fish was that had gotten away, a waitress passed. His hand hit a glass of ale she was carrying on a tray and some of the dark brew spilled on the white wall of the pub. It began to run down. The waitress hastily took a cloth from her apron and began to wipe, but the ale had left an ugly dark stain.

At another table, a man rose and came over. He took a crayon from his pocket and as all in the pub watched, began to sketch around the stain. In a few moments, he had drawn the head of a magnificent stag with spreading antlers. Under his hand, the mistake had become a thing of beauty. The artist was Sir Edwin Landseer, at that time England's foremost painter of animals.

Mistakes occur in our lives and yet, it seems that there are always those who can take a mistake, turn it around, and make something good come from it.

MONEY ❖ ❖ ❖

It's good to have money and the things money can buy, but it's good to check once in a while and make sure you haven't lost the things that money can't buy.

GEORGE HORACE LORIMER

WHEN the Riviera United Methodist Church in Redondo Beach, California, needed more money than the Sunday collections were bringing in, the Rev. Orlie White remembered the biblical parable of the talents. Putting that parable into practice, Rev. White filled a collection plate with $10 bills and invited each of his 200 parishioners to take one. He asked them to use the money to make more money, then return the original $10 and the amount it had earned to the church.

One woman bought needles and yarn and crocheted covers for clothes hangers, which she sold for a profit of $38. Another used the money to enter a bowling tournament and won a $75 prize for the church. A man and his wife pooled their stake and bought a share of stock for $20; three months later, they sold it for more than $50.

By the end of the year, the original $2,000 had grown into $8,000.

Closet space is like money. You use up as much as you have.

RAY MICHEL

A good rule is not to talk about money with people who have much more or much less than you.

KATHARINE WHITEHORN

❖ ❖ ❖ MORALITY

If everybody obeyed the Ten Commandments there might not be an 11 o'clock news.

MICHAEL SOVERN resigned as president of Columbia University in 1993. A reporter asked Sovern if there were any task he had left incomplete.

"Yes," replied Sovern. "It sounds complacent, but there is really only one." He referred to the lack of instruction in ethics. Professional schools, he pointed out, like law, medical, and business administration, have some pretty good programs in values and professional ethics. The average undergraduate, however, gets no training in these areas.

Why? Most likely because most educators—from grammar school through college—are afraid to touch the subjects. Topics such as these are usually addressed by parents or members of religious organizations. The result is that in this country, young people who need moral and ethical training more than ever are getting less than ever.

Morals and ethics are *not* a religion. They are logical, sensible principles of good conduct that we need for a peaceful, productive society.

When Thomas Jefferson created the state-run University of Virginia, he insisted that it have no religious affiliation. Yet even with this restriction, he still included "moral philosophy" in the required course of study.

Shouldn't we teach good morals and ethics not as religion, but simply as the most practical, direct route to success and happiness? And hadn't we better do it soon?

JOHN L. BECKLEY

Society is divided into two groups when it comes to the morality of our actions. One group says, "What's the harm?" while the other says, "What's the good?" Sanity and the continuation of civilization rest with the latter group.

MOTHERS ✦ ✦ ✦

A BOY was trying to figure out what to buy for his girlfriend's birthday. Finally, he asked his mother for some advice. "If you were going to be 16 years old tomorrow, what would you want?"

"Not another thing," his mother said without hesitation.

A YOUNG WOMAN named Mary gave birth to her first child and because her husband was on military duty, she spent a couple of weeks after the birth at the home of her parents.

One day Mary mentioned to her mother that she was surprised the baby's hair was reddish when both she and her husband were blonde.

"Well Mary," said the grandmother, "you must remember, your daddy's hair is red."

"But Mamma," said Mary, "that doesn't make any difference, because I'm adopted."

With a little smile, Mamma said the loveliest words that her daughter had ever heard: "I always forget."

All mothers are physically handicapped. They have only two hands.

IT WAS one of mother's hectic days. Her small son, who had been playing outside, came in with his pants torn. "You go right in, remove those pants, and start mending them yourself," she ordered.

Some time later she went to see how he was getting along. The torn pants were lying across the chair, and the door to the cellar, usually kept closed, was open. She called down the stairs, loudly and sternly:

"Are you running around down there without your pants on?"

"No, ma'am," was the deep-voiced reply. "I'm just down here reading your gas meter."

BEING A WORKING WOMAN can be tough, but holding a job and having children is even tougher.

There's a story about a mother with three active boys who were playing cops and robbers in the backyard after dinner one summer evening.

One of the boys "shot" his mother and yelled, "Bang, you're dead." She slumped to the ground and when she didn't get up right away, a neighbor ran over to see if she had been hurt in the fall.

When the neighbor bent over, the overworked mother opened one eye and said, "Shhh. Don't give me away. It's the only chance I get to rest."

A BUSINESSMAN was telling his mother about his Concorde flight from London to New York, which had taken only about three hours.

"For that much money," his mother said, "they should have let you ride a little longer."

MOTIVATION ❖ ❖ ❖

THERE ONCE WAS A DOG who boasted to his canine friends that he could run faster than anyone. One day he chased a rabbit and failed to catch it. His friends ridiculed him.

"All right," said the dog, "I did not make good on my boast. But remember, the rabbit was running for his life and I was only running for my dinner."

Incentive is all-important in motivation.

There is only one way to get anybody to do anything . . . . That is by making the other person *want* to do it. There is no other way.

DALE CARNEGIE

❖ ❖ ❖ PATIENCE

Patience is power; with time and patience the mulberry leaf becomes silk.

CHINESE PROVERB

Patience is a bitter plant that produces sweet fruit.

The great pianist and composer, Ignacy Paderewski, was once asked by an admirer how he had reached such a state of perfection in his field. It must have involved a lot of patience, the admirer remarked.

"Everyone has patience," said Paderewski. "I learned to use mine."

If you are patient in one moment of anger, you will escape a hundred days of sorrow.

❖ ❖ ❖ PERFECTION

MICHELANGELO was once putting what appeared to be the finishing touches on a sculpture when a friend dropped in for a visit. Days later, the friend dropped by again and was surprised to find the artist still working on the same statue.

The statue looked the same to the friend as it had days earlier, so he said, "You haven't been working on this statue all this time, have you?"

"I have," Michelangelo replied. "I've been busy retouching this part, and polishing that part; I've softened this feature, and brought out that muscle; I've given more expression to the lips, and more energy to that arm."

"But all those things are so insignificant," said the friend. "They're mere trifles."

"That may be so," replied Michelangelo, "but trifles make perfection, and perfection is no trifle."

PERSEVERANCE ❖ ❖ ❖

FIGHT ONE MORE ROUND. When your feet are so tired that you have to shuffle back to the center of the ring, fight one more round. When your arms are so tired that you can hardly lift your hands to come on guard, fight one more round. When your nose is bleeding and your eyes are black and you are so tired that you wish your opponent would crack you one on the jaw and put you to sleep, fight one more round—remembering that the man who always fights one more round is never whipped.

JAMES J. CORBETT

WILMA RUDOLPH certainly didn't get any head start in life. She was the 20th of 22 children born into a poor family in Tennessee. In childhood she fell victim to polio and was forced to wear leg braces until she was nine. At the age of 12 she tried out for her school's girl's basketball team. She failed. But for the next year she practiced virtually every day with a girlfriend and two neighborhood boys. Next time around, she made the team. It soon became evident that she could get from one end of the basketball court to the other quicker than anyone. A college track coach spotted her and talked her into letting him train her to be a sprinter. Her prowess earned her a scholarship to Tennessee State University where she became a track star.

In 1960, she made the U.S. Olympic team. In the 100-meter sprint she had to face Yetta Mynie of the German team. Yetta was unbeaten and the world record holder in that event. Wilma won. She did it again in the 200-meter event. Wilma's third race was in the 400-meter relay, in which she ran the anchor leg. Yetta Mynie was also running the last leg. Just as the baton was handed to Wilma, she dropped it, giving Yetta the lead. Her never-give-up spirit made her pick up the baton and take off in desperate pursuit. She caught the German champion in the last few strides and won a third gold medal, more than any other woman had at that time.

Today, Wilma Rudolph is a grandmother who travels the world as a spokesperson for various children's causes, motivating them with her life story.

"I let them know," she says, "that they can achieve, that they can grasp anything they want to grasp as long as they are willing to work for it."

PHYLLIS DILLER, the famous comedienne, has her own formula for success—she believes she can accomplish anything she sets out to do. "Life is a do-it-yourself kit," she laughs. "Believing in your- self completely is imperative."

She didn't always think that way. Before her public life began, she was a housewife with five children and a $50-a-week part-time job. Then she read a book that emphasized the impor- tance of positive thinking, of *believing* you can do something. Gradually she turned her negative thoughts about her abilities into positive ones. It took two years to complete the process.

Phyllis started by setting goals for herself. Her first one was to write a funny book. She accomplished that goal, then wrote two more and set out to become a performing comic. She volunteered to perform for charities, gradually steeling up her courage to go on stage. After four years of hard work and dedication to improving herself, her name was made in show business.

But Phyllis didn't stop there. She had studied music and always wanted to become a concert pianist. Once again, she set her goals and has appeared as guest soloist with many of the country's leading symphony orchestras. "Once I made up my mind," she says, "it was merely a matter of setting goals and reaching them. I started with a little acorn that grew into an oak."

Saints are sinners who kept on trying.

Perseverance is not a long race; it is many short races one after another.

WALTER ELLIOTT

WHEN he was a child, Winston Churchill was almost totally rejected by preoccupied, disinterested parents. He wrote innumerable letters from boarding school pleading with his mother to visit him at Christmas. The letters either went unanswered or the replies failed to refer to any plans about the family getting together at Christmas. When all the other students left the school to be with their families during the holidays, young Winston remained alone at his school.

It's astounding that with his incredibly unfortunate childhood—coupled with a continued series of failures at school and later, political failure upon failure—that Churchill would show such greatness in his country's finest hour.

But late in his life, he said something that gives us some insight into his greatness. He was 80 years old when he was asked to give the commencement address at Harrow, the boarding school he had attended as a youth. He stood up, looked over his glasses at the young graduates, and delivered one of the shortest commencement addresses on record.

"Never, never, never give up!" he cried out.

With that he sat down.

Tenacity is a pretty fair substitute for bravery, and the best form of tenacity I know is expressed in a Danish fur trapper's principle: *"The next mile is the only one a person really has to make."*

ERIC SEVAREID

In 1914 Thomas Edison's factory in West Orange, New Jersey, was virtually destroyed by fire. Although the damage exceeded $2 million, the buildings were insured for only $238,000 because they were made of concrete and were thought to be fireproof. Much of Edison's life's work went up in smoke and flames that December night.

At the height of the fire, Edison's 24-year-old son, Charles, searched frantically for his father. He finally found him, calmly watching the fire, his face glowing in the reflection, his white hair blowing in the wind.

"My heart ached for him," said Charles. "He was 67—no longer a young man—and everything was going up in flames. When he saw me, he shouted, 'Charles, where's your mother?' When I told him I didn't know, he said, 'Find her. Bring her here. She will never see anything like this as long as she lives.' "

The next morning, Edison looked at the ruins and said, "There is great value in disaster. All our mistakes are burned up. Thank God we can start anew."

Three weeks after the fire, Edison managed to deliver the first phonograph.

WHATEVER YOUR OCCUPATION is, you should work hard at it and enjoy it.

"Take it," said Mark Twain, "just as though it was, as it is, an earnest, vital, and important affair. Take it as though you were born to the task of performing a merry part of it, as though the world awaited your coming. Take it as though it was a grand opportunity to do and achieve, to carry forward great and good schemes, to help and cheer the suffering, the weary, the heart-broken.

"Now and then someone stands aside from the crowd, labors earnestly, steadfastly, and confidently, and straightaway becomes famous for wisdom, intellect, skill, or greatness of some sort. The world wonders, admires, idolizes, and it only illustrates what others may do if they take hold of life with a purpose. The miracle or the power that elevates the few is to be found in their industry, application, and perseverance under the inner promptings of a brave and determined spirit."

OUR FAVORITE FOOTBALL STORY came out of the game between the Detroit Lions and the New Orleans Saints in November 1970.

The outcome was decided in the final few seconds. The Saints had the ball but were a long way from the goal line. There was time for just one more play and the crowd gasped when they realized that the Saints were going to try a field goal of 63 yards—something that had never been done before.

The kicker was no Goliath, but he was unusual, even though some people didn't know it. He had no toes on his right foot and only half of his kicking foot. There were no fingers on his right hand. But that didn't stop Tom Dempsey. He gave it everything he had and the kick was good. The beautiful thing about it was not that Tom Dempsey won a football game, but that he did what he had been doing all his life. He accomplished something against great odds because he refused to be stopped by his disability.

NOTHING IN THIS WORLD can take the place of persistence. Talent will not; nothing is more common than unsuccessful people with talent. Genius will not; unrewarded genius is almost a proverb. Education will not; the world is full of educated derelicts. Persistence and determination alone are omnipotent. The slogan "press on" has solved and always will solve the problems of the human race.

CALVIN COOLIDGE

❖ ❖ ❖ **PERSPECTIVE**

WHEN DEALING WITH PEOPLE, it is important to remember that everyone does not see things from the same perspective. Understanding someone's viewpoint is the first step to effective communication. Unfortunately, the perspective of others is too often overlooked.

When I think of perspective I am often reminded of a conversation between me and my son in the summer he turned four. That spring Mark had asked for a spot in the family garden to call his own. He turned the soil, broke the clumps, and planted his favorite vegetable—corn.

Toward the middle of July, Mark was concerned that his corn was not growing fast enough. I tried to reassure him that the corn was doing just fine by quoting him the familiar benchmark used by farmers, ". . . knee-high by the Fourth of July." My lesson came with his retort: "My knees or yours?"

NICHOLAS MOKELKE

TO PLEASE HIS FATHER, a freshman went out for track. He had no athletic ability, though the father had been a good miler in his day. His first race was a two-man race in which he ran against the school miler. He was badly beaten.

Not wanting to disappoint his father, the boy wrote home as follows: "You will be happy to know that I ran against Bill Williams, the best miler in school. He came in next to last, while I came in second."

SO MUCH DEPENDS on one's point of view.

Back near the turn of the century, a statue of General William Tecumseh Sherman was erected in Washington, D. C., outside the U.S. Treasury. To Northerners, Sherman was a military hero. To the South, even at that time he remained a symbol of the defeat and degradation suffered by the Confederacy, and he was hated by Southerners as the man who had devastated Georgia from Atlanta to the sea.

The task of unveiling the monument to Sherman fell to Lyman J. Gage, who was then secretary of the treasury. He approached this duty with mixed emotions, but the event passed without incident.

When the ceremony was over, Gage talked to a southern newspaper correspondent and asked him what he thought about the monument.

"Well, Mr. Secretary," the correspondent said, "from the north side where we stand, you see General Sherman as a soldier and gentleman astride his mighty charger. But from the south side all you can see is what we have always seen—a horse's rear end."

♦ ♦ ♦ **PERSUASION**

EVERYBODY but Sam had signed up for a new company pension plan that called for a small employee contribution. The company was paying all the rest.

Unfortunately, 100 percent employee participation was needed; otherwise the plan was off.

Sam's boss and his fellow workers pleaded and cajoled, but to no avail. Sam said the plan would never pay off.

Finally the company president called Sam into his office. "Sam," he said, "here's a copy of the new pension plan and here's a pen. I want you to sign the papers. I'm sorry, but if you don't sign, you're fired. As of right now."

Sam signed the papers immediately.

"Now," said the president, "would you mind telling me why you couldn't have signed earlier?"

"Well, sir," replied Sam, "nobody explained it to me quite so clearly before."

♦ ♦ ♦ **POLICE**

THE NEW MAYOR called in the police chief of the small town and talked about the area and the size of the force. "How many police officers do you have?"

"There's me, the chief of police, and I have six other officers."

"In a small town like this, surely there's not enough crime to keep a police force of seven people busy," said the mayor.

"That's true," said the chief. "But if we didn't have seven officers, there would be."

PRAGMATISM ❖ ❖ ❖

WHEN THE CIVIL WAR ENDED, some people were clamoring for the capture and hanging of Jefferson Davis, head of the Confederacy.

President Abraham Lincoln, eager to heal the nation's wounds as soon as possible, felt there were good reasons to resist these demands, but it was not politic for him to come out and say it.

Finally, General Sherman met with Lincoln and asked whether the President wanted him to capture Davis or let him escape.

"Let me tell you what I think of taking Jeff Davis," Lincoln replied. "Out in Sangamon County there was an old temperance lecturer who was very strict in the doctrine and practice of total abstinence. One day, after a long ride in the hot sun, he stopped at the house of a friend, who proposed making him a lemonade. As it was being mixed the friend asked if he wouldn't like a drop of something stronger to brace his nerves after the exhausting heat and exercise.

" 'No,' said the lecturer, 'I wouldn't think of it. I'm opposed to it on principle, but if you could manage to put in a drop unbeknownst to me, I guess it wouldn't hurt me much.'

"Now, General," Lincoln said, "I am bound to oppose the escape of Jeff Davis, but if you could manage to let him slip out, unbeknownstlike, I guess it wouldn't hurt me much."

❖ ❖ ❖   PRAISE

Praise does wonders for the sense of hearing.

"ONE THING scientists have discovered," notes Thomas Dreier, "is that often-praised children become more intelligent than often-blamed ones. There's a *creative element* in praise."

Good leaders know that, fundamentally, their job is to help others make the most of themselves. Viewed in strictly commercial terms, that is their greatest contribution to their companies. People, employees, are a great untapped reservoir of energy. Leaders who can tap this source are valuable to any organization.

None of us likes to have his or her work taken for granted. Yet it can easily happen these days under the pressure of everyday business, especially when a person's contribution gets blurred into a large effort and becomes impossible to identify.

This is one of the major psychological problems of big business and mass production industries. When people get the impression that their jobs and their work don't really matter, the quality of their efforts tends to slump sharply.

It doesn't take elaborate incentives to bring out the best in people. If you recognize their work—make them feel like holding their heads up because their jobs and the way they do them count for something—they'll usually give you the best that's in them.

PRAYER ❖ ❖ ❖

Lord, when we are wrong, make us willing to change. And when we are right, make us easy to live with.

PETER MARSHALL

A Prayer for Today

This is the beginning of a new day.

God has given me this day to use as I will.

I can waste it or use it for good, but what I do today is important, because I am exchanging a day of my life for it.

When tomorrow comes, this day will be gone forever, leaving in its place something that I have traded for it.

I want it to be gain, and not loss; good, and not evil; success, and not failure, in order that I shall not regret the price I have paid for it.

This day is all we have. Is there someone to whom an act of kindness—not tomorrow but today—could make a world of difference?

Today, whether we spend it well or throw it away, will be gone tomorrow. What is there to do that is worth our effort?

W. HEARTSILL WILSON

PEOPLE WHO PRAY FOR MIRACLES usually don't get miracles . . . . But people who pray for courage, for strength to bear the unbearable, for the grace to remember what they have left instead of what they have lost, very often find their prayers answered. Their

144

prayers helped them tap hidden reserves of faith and courage that were not available to them before.

HAROLD S. KUSHNER

❖ ❖ ❖ **PREPARATION**

A BASEBALL COACH once rebuked a confident player who said their team would win because it had "the will to win."

"Don't kid yourself," said the coach. "The will to win is important, but it isn't worth a nickel unless you also have the will to prepare."

The best preparation for tomorrow is to do today's work superbly well.

SIR WILLIAM OSLER

TV NEWSCASTER Morton Dean learned a valuable lesson early in life.

"I did a lot of bench time as a high school football player," he recalls. "And I remember being called off the bench suddenly during one game when my team was a yard and a half from the goal line. I was a reserve quarterback and hadn't played yet that season. But we used a very simple, basic offense, and I think the coach thought this was a good chance for me to go in. He wanted me to achieve something so that I could build up my confidence. So he said, 'Throw a jump pass.'

"For us, that goal-line play just meant stepping back, jump-

145

ing up, and popping the ball to the end. It would have been a touchdown—on my very first play."

Well, what did our hero do?

"I ran in, got the ball, fumbled it, and fell on it. I've had nightmares about this ever since. My father had always said, *ad nauseam*, 'You've got to be prepared to come off the bench.' But that day, I wasn't prepared."

Ever since that experience, Dean has always tried to be ready for any eventuality. "In the television news business," he says, "a lot of people try to pretend that they just come on without any preparation and do it perfectly. But it doesn't work that way. You have to do your homework. It ain't that easy."

Heed his advice. Do your homework. Prepare for the unexpected. Learn all you can before you plunge into a task. It's a lesson all successful people have learned.

———————

Fred Astaire once said something about his dance routines that could be applied to speech making, storytelling, and a lot of other things. He said, "Get it 'til it's perfect, then cut two minutes."

PRIDE ❖ ❖ ❖

Temper gets you into trouble. Pride keeps you there.

———————

A CROWD watched a peacock spread its tail and show its dazzling plumage one day in a park zoo. The bird drew oohs and ahs from the people as it strutted regally about its pen. Then a dull-brown duck waddled between the peacock and the crowd. The peacock became angry and drove the duck back into a nearby pond. In its rage, the peacock's tail closed like a fan and the bird seemed ugly.

But the duck began swimming and diving gracefully in the pond and no longer seemed unattractive. Those who had been singing the praises of the peacock now loved the duck.

As the adages put it: *Pride goeth before a fall,* and *true happiness comes from being yourself.*

❖ ❖ ❖ PROBLEMS

A BUSINESSMAN who was having a lot of financial problems scraped together enough money to attend the 25th reunion of his high school class. There he met a good friend who was obviously *not* having financial problems. The friend arrived in an expensive car. He wore expensive clothes and from all reports was a grand success in the airline business.

"Jim," said the man with all the problems, "I've got to hand it to you. You really made something of yourself and I'm really happy for you. But, tell me, how did it happen?"

"Bill," replied Jim, "it all came about because I got religion. After high school, I had an ordinary job in a factory, but one day I met a girl. We got married and I began going to church every Sunday. And because of that, I began to read the Bible. I used to just open up the Bible, put my finger on a page, and begin to read. One day I opened it up and put my finger on the word *bull*. It so happened that we went to the state fair the next day and they were selling tickets on a prize bull. We won the bull and we got a loan from the bank so we could buy a little farm and keep the bull. We planned to raise cattle. Then one day I opened my Bible and put my finger on the word *oil*. I talked to some people and wound up in a deal with a man who drilled wildcat oil wells. He thought there might be oil on my property, so we got enough money together to drill a well and it turned out to be a tremendous gusher. We bought a lot of adjoining property and discovered more oil. Finally, one day I opened my Bible and put my finger on the word *wings*. The next day I bought this little airline and today I have the biggest commuter airline in the country."

Bill listened to all this and could hardly wait to get back to his motel room. As soon as he got in the door, he found the Gideon Bible, opened it up, closed his eyes, and put his finger on the page. "Lord, tell me what to do," he whispered. Then he opened his eyes, looked down to where his finger was pointing and read *Chapter 11*.

A problem well stated is a problem half solved.

CHARLES KETTERING

A long dispute means that both parties are wrong.

A SMALL TROUBLE is like a pebble. Hold it too close to your eye and it fills the whole world and puts everything out of focus. Hold it at a proper distance and it can be examined and properly classified. Throw it at your feet and it can be seen in its true setting, just one more tiny bump on the pathway of life.

CELIA LUCE

The next best thing to solving a problem is finding some humor in it.

The best way to forget your own problems is to help others solve theirs.

A WOMAN EXECUTIVE on a coast-to-coast flight was trying to get some work done but was having a problem concentrating because a four-year-old boy was noisily running up and down the aisles.

At one point, he hit the keys of someone's calculator, voiding a half hour's work. He spilled another person's cup of coffee, awakened a snoozing passenger, and generally created havoc.

One passenger finally insisted that the boy be strapped into his seat. But when it was done, his screams were worse than his antics.

After this went on for a while the woman executive summoned a flight attendant and whispered into her ear. The attendant nodded and disappeared into the pilot's compartment.

"What did you say to her?" a nearby passenger asked.

"I suggested," said the executive, "that instead of trying to solve *our* problem with this little guy, we ought to try to solve *his* problem."

A minute later, the pilot came out of the cockpit and asked the boy if he would like to fly the airplane. The boy was soon sitting on the pilot's lap, "flying" the rest of the way. Not a peep was heard from him again.

PROCRASTINATION ❖ ❖ ❖

If you put off doing an easy job, it only makes the job harder. If you put off doing a hard job, it makes it impossible.

One of these days is none of these days.

The longer you wait to write a thank-you note, the longer it must be.

PRODUCTION ❖ ❖ ❖

A CONTRACTOR was driven almost crazy by the slow pace of his workers on a construction project. They were being paid by the day to haul dirt to a dump with wheelbarrows.

After figuring out what it was costing for each wheelbarrow load, he got an idea. He instructed the foreman to stand at the dump with a supply of money. The workers would be paid on the spot for each load delivered.

The change worked. The pace picked up to the point that the job was finished in little more than half the time allotted, and at considerable savings.

ONE MAN challenged another to an all-day wood chopping contest.

The challenger worked very hard, stopping only for a brief lunch break. The other man had a leisurely lunch and took several breaks during the day. At the end of the day, the challenger was surprised and annoyed to find that the other fellow had chopped substantially more wood than he had.

"I don't get it," he said. "Every time I checked, you were taking a rest, yet you chopped more wood than I did."

"But you didn't notice," said the winning woodsman, "that when I sat down to rest, I was sharpening my ax."

———————

A COMPANY was having trouble with its internal mail deliveries and one day the boss decided to personally take a look at the mail room operation.

He went there expecting to find a group of workers goofing off. But the first thing that caught his eye was a young fellow who looked like a magician doing card tricks. Envelopes flew out of his hands into the various distribution slots. And as he worked, he whistled, sang, and laughed. He was a shining example of a happy, ambitious, and efficient employee.

"Excuse me, son," said the boss. "I am the president of this company and I want to commend you on the way you work."

"Thank you, sir, but this isn't work to me," said the young fellow. "I think it's fun."

"Oh, I'd give anything to have more people with that attitude," said the boss. "When you think a job is fun, you do it better. You're certainly proof of that! I've never seen anyone sort mail as fast as you do."

"You haven't seen anything yet," said the young man. "Wait until you see how fast I am after I learn how to read."

———————

The best way to get relief from a monotonous task is to think of ways to improve it.

———————

We REMEMBER a house along the Delaware River in New York State that had a hand pump in the kitchen to bring water in from a surface spring out in the yard. There was always a jar filled with water in the kitchen. When you wanted more water, you poured a little from the jar into the pump to prime it to get it going. As long as you pumped, the water kept coming. When you stopped pumping, the water flow stopped too.

Some people are like that. You have to prime and pump them. If you want them to do something, you have to get them started and practically pull the effort out of them.

There's another type of well—the artesian well. You create an artesian well by boring into the earth until you reach a water level that has internal pressure. The pressure pushes the water up. All you have to do is put a pipe into the well, extend it to your kitchen faucet and you're in business. Just turn on the faucet and the water flows.

There are people like *that* also. Ask them to do something and they respond immediately. They don't have to be primed. They don't have to be pumped.

The difference is that some are always ready to produce while some are not. Some are shallow and some are deep.

PROGRESS ❖ ❖ ❖

INTREPID HUNTERS Luke and Anton hired a seaplane to take them hunting in the Canadian wilds. They were to fly in at sunrise and fly out at sunset.

All went well on the way in, but when the pilot returned to pick them up, he found Luke, Anton, and two large moose.

"You'll have to leave one of those moose behind," the pilot said. "I can't handle the weight."

"No way!" cried Luke. "Last year we chartered a plane just like yours, and the pilot took us *and* two moose."

"Hmmm," mused the pilot, "I'm the best there is, and if he did it last year I can do it today. Let's load up!"

They loaded both moose, Luke and Anton, their gear, and the pilot. The little plane roared down the lake, struggling to gain altitude, barely clearing the treetops. The pilot managed to keep the plane airborne for a while but the weight proved too much. The little plane plopped down on an adjoining lake.

Anton looked around and saw no one was hurt. Turning to Luke he asked, "How did we do?"

"Pretty good," said Luke. "I think we got a few miles farther than last year."

The Jokesmith

♦ ♦ ♦ **PROMISES**

If asked when you can deliver something, ask for time to think. Build in a margin of safety. Name a date. Then deliver it earlier than you promised. The world is divided into two classes of people: the few people who make good on their promises (even if they don't promise as much), and the many who don't. Get in Column A and stay there. You'll be very valuable wherever you are.

ROBERT TOWNSEND

PSYCHOLOGY ❖ ❖ ❖

A WOMAN seeking counsel from Dr. George W. Crane, the psychologist, confided that she hated her husband, and intended to divorce him. "I want to hurt him all I can," she declared firmly.

"Well, in that case," said Dr. Crane, "I advise you to start showering him with compliments. When you have become indispensable to him, when he thinks you love him devotedly, then start the divorce action. That is the way to hurt him."

Some months later the wife returned to report that all was going well. She had followed the suggested course.

"Good," said Dr. Crane. "Now's the time to file for divorce."

"Divorce!" the woman said indignantly. "Never. I love my husband dearly!"

ACCORDING TO LEGEND, when Michelangelo started out, he was ignored by his own generation and disdained by art critics. But he had faith in his ability, and he decided to use some psychology on his critics.

He knew they were fascinated when someone excavated an old ruin and dug up a supposedly priceless work of art, so he stained one of his works and had it buried where an excavating party was sure to find it.

The critics were enraptured. They pronounced it a work of rare value. The Cardinal of San Giorgio was so impressed that he paid a large sum for it. Then Michelangelo let the cat out of the bag. The art critics had no choice but to admit that he was an artistic genius. After that, Michelangelo was commissioned to do important work.

❖ ❖ ❖ PUBLIC SPEAKING

A TOASTMASTER was asked to pay a tribute to the chairman of a volunteer organization at its annual banquet. The chairman hadn't been much more than a figurehead, and that made the toastmaster's task somewhat difficult, but this is what he said:

> Ladies and gentlemen, I think we all agree that we owe a great debt of gratitude to our chairman, who has presided so capably in the chair of this organization. His unique abilities bring to mind a bit of Irish folklore.
>
> The Irish believe that a leprechaun kisses every baby that is born. If the kiss is on the brow, the child is destined to become an intellectual. If the kiss is on the eyes, the child will become a great beauty; if on the fingers, a great artist.
>
> Now, I am not in a position to tell you where the leprechaun kissed Mr. Clark, but you will have to admit he makes a wonderful chairman.

How much it adds to human grief
That witty speech is often brief.
How true it is—and what a pity
That lengthy talks are seldom witty.

Public speaking is like taking a vacation. It helps to know the right place to stop.

WINSTON CHURCHILL was said to have used a simple trick to make people believe that he did his public speaking without a text in front of him. The fact is, he read virtually all his speeches, but he always used a few quotations in the body of his speech. When he got to a quote, he would put on his eyeglasses to make it appear that he needed them to read.

New York Governor Mario Cuomo once led off a speech with this remark: "They told me not to be witty or intellectual; just be myself."

POET LOUIS UNTERMEYER once gave a talk to a small group that could ill afford to pay his fee. When he became aware that the group was struggling financially, he returned his fee and asked that the money be put to good use.

Some time later he ran into a member of the group and asked to what good use the money had been put.

"We started a fund to get better speakers next year," was the reply.

One thing a speaker should remember for sure; the mind can absorb only what the seat can endure.

QUALITY ❖ ❖ ❖

People may forget how fast you did a job, but they will remember how well you did it.

GET THE CONFIDENCE of the public and you will have no difficulty in getting their patronage. Inspire your whole force with the right spirit of service; encourage every sign of the true spirit. So display and advertise wares that customers shall buy with understanding. Treat them as guests when they come and when they go, whether or not they buy. Give them all that can be given fairly, on the principle that to him that giveth shall be given. Remember always that the recollection of quality remains long after the price is forgotten. Then your business will prosper by a natural process.

H. GORDON SELFRIDGE

IF A THING IS OLD, it is a sign that it was fit to live. Old families, old customs, old styles survive because they are fit to survive. The guarantee of continuity is quality. Submerge the good in a flood of the new, and the good will come back bigger than ever. Old-fashioned hospitality, old-fashioned politeness, old-fashioned honor in business had qualities of survival. These will come back.

Quantity is what you can count. **Quality** is what you can count on.

A YOUNG EXECUTIVE bought a house in the country. She also bought a horse, then went looking for a place to board it because she didn't have a barn. In the process she learned an old lesson: You get what you pay for.

The first neighbor she approached said he would keep the horse for $25 a day, plus the manure. Some people wanted the manure for their gardens, he explained, and he could use it on his farm.

Another neighbor's price was $15 a day, plus manure.

157

She checked with a third farmer and he offered to board the horse for $5 a day.

"What about the manure?" the horse owner asked.

"For $5 a day there won't be any," replied the farmer.

RESPONSIBILITY ❖ ❖ ❖

SOMEONE ONCE SAID that good leaders take a little more than their share of the blame and a little less than their share of the credit.

That's clear in this Civil War story about Abraham Lincoln.

After the Battle of Gettysburg, General Robert E. Lee and his Confederate forces were withdrawing to Virginia, and Lincoln felt that they were vulnerable. Eager to get the agony of the war over with, President Lincoln sent word to General George Meade to attack.

With his message, Lincoln also sent a personal note. "The order I enclose is not on record," said the note. "If you succeed, you need not publish it. Then, if you succeed, you will have all the credit of the movement. If not, I'll take the responsibility."

THE CELEBRATED HISTORIAN Barbara Tuchman called our times *"The Age of Disruption,* a period when we've lost belief in certain kinds of moral understanding of good and bad."

A reporter for *The Indianapolis Star* once asked the two-time Pulitzer Prize winner what she thought was most needed in the next century.

"Probably *personal responsibility,"* she replied, explaining that this means "taking responsibility for your behavior and your expenditures and your actions, and not forever supposing that society must forgive you because it's not your fault."

◆ ◆ ◆ **RETIREMENT**

One retired man made beautiful toys in his workshop, and he sold them to a toy store. It was hard work.

A retired woman made beautiful dolls and she gave them away to poor children. It was a pleasure.

ODE TO RETIREMENT

Old age is golden, I've heard it said,
But sometimes I wonder as I get into bed—
With my ears in a drawer, my teeth in a cup,
My eyes on the table until I wake up.

Ere sleep dims my eyes, I say to myself,
"Is there anything else I should lay on the shelf?"
And I'm happy to say as I close my door,
"My friends are the same, only perhaps even more!"

When I was young, my slippers were red—
I could kick my heels right over my head.
When I grew older, my slippers were blue—
But I still could dance the whole night through.
Now I am old, my slippers are black;
I walk to the store—and puff my way back!

The reason I know my youth is all spent?
My get up and go has got up and went.
But I really don't mind when I think, with a grin,
Of all the grand places my get up has been.

Since I have retired from Life's competition,
I busy myself with complete repetition:
I get up each morning and dust off my wits;
Pick up my paper and read the "Obits."
If my name is missing, I know I'm not dead;
So I eat a good breakfast—and go back to bed.

AUTHOR UNKNOWN

RISKS ❖ ❖ ❖

Behold the turtle; he makes progress only when he sticks his neck out.

These words by James Bryant Conant have special meaning for writer James Michener.

In 1944, when Michener was nearly 40, he was serving in the U.S. Navy on a remote island in the South Pacific. To kill time, he decided to write a book. He knew that the chances of anyone's publishing it were practically nil. But he decided to stick his neck out and give it a try.

Michener had decided that the book would be a collection of short stories. A friend told him that nobody publishes short stories anymore. Even so, he stuck his neck out and went ahead. The book was published and it got few reviews, but Orville Prescott, the book reviewer for *The New York Times*, reported that he liked the stories. Others decided they liked the book too, and it wound up winning a Pulitzer Prize.

Kenneth McKenna, whose job it was to evaluate books for a Hollywood film company, tried to persuade his company to make a movie out of it, but the company decided the book "had no dramatic possibilities." So McKenna stuck *his* neck out and brought the book to the attention of composers Richard Rodgers and Oscar Hammerstein II.

160

When Broadway cynics heard that Rodgers and Hammer-stein were planning a musical called *South Pacific*, they guffawed and said, "Have you heard about this screwy idea? The romantic lead is gonna be a guy past 50. An opera singer named Ezio Pinza!"

Everyone knows what happened after that. "You can understand," said Michener, "why I like people who stick their necks out."

❖ ❖ ❖ **RULES**

FROM THE RULE OF ST. BENEDICT, Sixth Century A.D.:

If any pilgrim monk come from distant parts, with wish as a guest to dwell in the monastery, and will be content with the customs which he finds in the place and not perchance by his lavishness disturb the monastery, but is simply content with what he finds, he shall be received, for as long a time as he desires. If, indeed, he find fault with anything, or expose it reasonably and with the humility of charity, the Abbot shall discuss it prudently, lest perchance God has sent him for this very thing. But if he have been found gossipy and contumacious in the time of his sojourn as guest, not only ought he not to be joined to the body of the monastery, but also it shall be said to him, honestly, that he must depart. If he does not go, let two stout monks, in the name of God, explain the matter to him.

❖ ❖ ❖ **SACRIFICE**

LATE IN THE 15TH CENTURY, two young wood-carving apprentices in France confided to each other their desire to study painting. But such study would take money, and both Hans and Albrecht were poor.

Finally, though, they had a solution. Let one work and earn money while the other studied. Then, when the lucky one became rich and famous, let him in turn aid the other. They tossed a coin and Albrecht won.

So while Albrecht went to Venice, Hans worked as a blacksmith. As quickly as he received his wages he would forward money to his friend.

The months stretched into years—and at last Albrecht returned to his native land, an independent master. Now it was his turn to help Hans.

The two men met in joyous reunion, but when Albrecht looked at his friend tears welled from his eyes. Only then did he discover the extent of Hans' sacrifice. The many years of heavy labor in the blacksmith shop had calloused and bruised Hans' sensitive hands. His fingers could never handle a painter's brush.

In humble gratitude to Hans for his years of sacrifice, the artist, the great Albrecht Dürer, painted a portrait of the work-worn hands that had labored so faithfully in order that he might develop his talent. He presented this painting of praying hands to his devoted friend. It has since become familiar to millions of people.

SALES/SELLING ♦ ♦ ♦

You can't just sell products. You have to sell benefits and solutions.

ONE SALESCLERK in a candy store always had customers lined up waiting while other salesclerks stood around with nothing to do. The owner of the store noted her popularity and asked for her secret. "It's easy," she said. "The others scoop up more than a pound of candy and then start taking away. I always scoop up less than a pound and then add to it."

MOTIVATIONAL SPEAKER Bill Gove tells a story about Harry, who ran a small appliance store in Phoenix, Arizona.

Harry was used to price-shopping by young couples. They would ask detailed questions about features, prices, and model numbers, and one of them always took notes. Harry knew that as soon as they left the store they were going to head for one of the discount appliance dealers to make comparisons. Nevertheless, Harry would patiently answer all their questions, even though it took more than a half hour at times. But when the couple would announce that they were going to look around at some other places, Harry had a standard spiel to deliver.

"I know that you're looking for the best deal you can find," he would say. "I understand that, because I do the same thing myself. I know you'll probably go down to Discount Dan's to compare prices. I know I would. But after you've done that, I want you to think of one thing. When you buy from Discount Dan's, you get an appliance—a good one, I know, because he sells the same appliances we do. But when you buy here, you get one thing you don't get at Dan's. You get me. I come with the deal. I stand behind what I sell. I want you to be happy with what you buy. I've been here 30 years. I learned the business from my Dad, and I hope to be able to give the business over to my daughter and son-in-law in a few years.

"So you know one thing for sure—when you buy an appliance from me, you get me with the deal. That means I'll do everything I can to be sure you never regret doing business with me. That's a guarantee."

Harry would then wish the couple well and give them a quart of ice cream in appreciation of their stopping at his store.

This is how Bill Gove finishes the story: "Now," he says, "how far do you think that couple is going to get, with Harry's speech ringing in their ears and a quart of ice cream on their hands in Phoenix, when it's 110 degrees in the shade?"

A storekeeper in Maine refused to buy a salesman's wares. "You must remember, young fellow," he said, "that in this part of the country every want ain't a need."

THE CHIEF BUYER for a thriving company was particularly inaccessible to salespeople. You didn't call *him*. He called *you*. On several occasions when salespeople managed to get into his office, they were summarily tossed out.

One saleswoman finally broke through his defenses. She sent him a homing pigeon with her card attached to one leg. On the card she had written, "If you want to know more about our product, just throw our representative out the window."

SECRETS ❖ ❖ ❖

A WELL-KNOWN JOURNALIST was dining at a four-star restaurant and she asked for the recipe for the entree she had ordered—lemon sole in a wonderful sauce. The waiter conferred with the head waiter, who conferred with the chef, who conferred with the proprietor.

The proprietor came to the woman's table and said, "I'm sorry, madame, but we have the same policy here as you journalists. We never reveal our sauces."

❖ ❖ ❖ SELF-IMPROVEMENT

COMEDIAN BRIAN KILEY went to a bookstore and asked the woman behind the counter where the self-help section was.

"If I told you," the woman said, "that would defeat the whole purpose."

———

Let me be a little kinder,
Let me be a little blinder
To the faults of those about me,
Let me praise a little more.

Let me be, when I am weary,
Just a little bit more cheery;
Let me serve a little better
Those whom I am working for.

Let me be a little braver
When temptation makes me waver;
Let me strive a little harder
To be all that I should be.

Let me be a little meeker
With the person who is weaker;
Let me think more of my neighbor
And a little less of me.

———

THERE'S A STORY about an executive who often dropped whatever change she had in a cup held by an amputee who sat on the street outside her office building. But she always insisted on getting one of the pencils the legless man had in a cup beside him.

"You're a businessman," she would say, "and I always expect to get good value from the people I do business with."

One day the amputee was not on the sidewalk. Time went by and the executive forgot about him. Then, many months later, she was on her way to get her train when she discovered the amputee running the newsstand in the terminal.

"I always hoped you'd come by some day," he said. "More than anyone else you're responsible for my being here. You kept telling me I was a businessman and I started thinking of myself that way. You gave me self-respect and that made me look at myself differently. One thing led to another, and here I am."

———————

If you're not working on yourself, you're not working.

SERVICE ❖ ❖ ❖

SOME BELIEVE there is nothing one man or one woman can do against the enormous array of the world's ills. Yet many of the world's great movements, of thought and action, have flowed from the work of a single person. A young monk began the Protestant Reformation, a young general extended an empire from Macedonia to the borders of the earth, and a young woman reclaimed the territory of France. It was a young Italian explorer who discovered the New World, and the 32-year-old Thomas Jefferson who proclaimed that all men are created equal.

These people moved the world, and so can we all. Few will have the greatness to bend history itself, but each of us can work to change a small portion of events, and in the total of all those acts will be written the history of this generation.

It is from numberless diverse acts of courage and belief that human history is shaped. Each time a person stands up for an ideal, or acts to improve the lot of others, or strikes out against injustice, he or she sends forth a tiny ripple of hope, and crossing each other from a million different centers of energy and daring, those ripples build a current that can sweep down the mightiest walls of oppression and resistance.

From an address by Robert Kennedy to the young people of South Africa on their Day of Affirmation in 1966.

❖ ❖ ❖ SHARING

YEARS AGO, near a seldom-used trail in the Amargosa Desert in California, there stood a rundown hut. Nearby was a well, the only source of water for miles around. Attached to the pump was a tin baking powder can with a message inside, written in pencil on a sheet of brown wrapping paper.

This was the message . . .

This pump is all right as of June 1932. I put a new sucker washer into it and it ought to last five years. But the washer dries out and the pump has got to be primed. Under the white rock I buried a bottle of water, out of the sun and cork end up. There's enough water in it to prime this pump but not if you drink some first. Pour in about 1/4 and let her soak to wet the leather. Then pour in the rest medium fast and pump like hell. You'll git water. The well never has ran dry. Have faith.

When you git watered up, fill the bottle and put it back like you found it for the next feller.

SIGNED: *Desert Pete*

P.S. Don't go drinking the water first! Prime the pump with it and you'll git all you can hold. And next time you pray, remember that God is like the pump. He has to be primed. I've given my last dime away a dozen times to prime the pump of my prayers, and

I've fed my last beans to a stranger while saying Amen. It never failed yet to git me an answer. You got to git your heart fixed to give before you can be give to.

A sorrow shared is half a trouble, but joy that's shared is joy made double.

ENGLISH PROVERB

GARDENERS know that many types of flowers will go to seed and die if blossoms are not picked regularly. If the flowers are picked before they begin to fade and dry up, more flowers will bloom and the plants will keep blooming throughout the summer, providing bouquets for friends and neighbors.

The same thing is true with other joys in life. If we keep them to ourselves they will dry up and die. If we share them with others they will multiply.

SIGNS ❖ ❖ ❖

SIGN in a Vermont bookshop:

We open Monday through Saturday at 9 a.m. Occasionally, if it's a real nice day, we open as early as 8:30. But some days, especially if it is raining, we don't open until 11. We close about 5 or 5:30. Occasionally, we close at 4:30, especially when the world seems dreary.

Sign on an office desk: *The buck pauses here and, having paused, moves on.*

AN ARMY CHAPLAIN posted the following sign on the door of his quarters:

If you have troubles, come in and tell us about them.

If not, come in and tell us how you do it.

SIGN outside a riding stable:

We have fast horses for folks who like to ride fast. We have slow horses for folks who ride slow. We have big horses for big folks, and we have little horses for little folks. And for those who have never ridden horses before, we have horses that have never been ridden.

Sign attached to the in-basket on a manager's desk: It has come to the attention of this desk that *too much* comes to the attention of this desk.

SIGN in a bookstore: *Browsers welcome, both high browse and low browse.*

SIGN in the window of an English company:

We have been established for over 100 years and have been pleasing and displeasing customers ever since. We have made money and lost money, suffered the effects of coal nationalization, coal rationing, government control, and bad payers. We have been cussed and discussed, messed about, lied to, held up, robbed, and swindled. The only reason we stay in business is to see what happens next.

SMILE ❖ ❖ ❖

A SMILE costs nothing, but it creates much.

It enriches those who receive it without impoverishing those who give it.

It happens in a flash, and the memory of it may last forever.

None are so rich that they can get along without it, and none so poor that they cannot be richer for its benefits.

It creates happiness in the home, fosters goodwill in a business, and is the countersign of friends.

It is rest to the weary, daylight to the discouraged, sunshine to the sad, and nature's best antidote for trouble.

Yet it cannot be begged, bought, borrowed, or stolen, for it is something that is worth nothing to anyone until it is given away.

In the course of the day, some of your acquaintances may be too tired to give you a smile. Give them one of yours.

Nobody needs a smile so much as those who have none left to give.

SOCIALISM ❖ ❖ ❖

BARON DE ROTHSCHILD of the European banking family once employed a valet who was sympathetic to the cause of socialism. He met regularly with a group that was pressing for socialist reforms. Baron de Rothschild had no particular concern about this, especially because the man was an excellent valet.

After some time, however, the Baron noted that the valet had stopped going to the meetings and he asked him if he had lost interest in the cause.

"Sir," said the valet, "at the last meeting I attended, someone got up and calculated that if all the wealth of France were divided equally, every individual would have 2,000 francs.

"Well, what about that?" said the Baron.

"Sir," said the valet, "I already have 5,000 francs."

❖ ❖ ❖ **SOLUTIONS**

IN BYGONE DAYS, a thin man insulted a fat man. The fat man challenged his tormentor to a duel with pistols.

On the day of the duel a debate ensued about the unfair advantage held by the thin man because he was a much smaller target. Finally the thin man came up with a solution.

"Let the outline of my figure be chalked upon your body," he said to his opponent, "and any shots of mine that hit outside the chalk lines, we won't count."

AN APPLE GROWER had built up a good mail-order business and was justifiably proud of his product. His apples were wonderful— crisp, juicy, bright red, and shiny as a carefully polished brass rail. His customers came to expect only the best in taste and appearance.

Then one year a hailstorm occurred just before the harvest. Nearly every apple was marred by hail.

The apple grower had thousands of orders and checks, and his customers were fully expecting baskets and boxes of his bountiful fruit for the holiday season. He had a problem. If he sent out the pockmarked fruit he would have thousands of dissatisfied customers and his business would suffer—perhaps even dry up.

The problem was in the appearance of the apples. How could he turn this liability into an asset?

The fact was, they tasted great. The taste was better than normal because cold weather improves the flavor of apples when they're approaching ripeness. So the grower decided to fill the orders he had. But with each shipment he enclosed a card that said, "Note the hail marks that have caused minor skin blemishes on some of these apples. They are proof of their growth at a high mountain altitude where the sudden chills from hailstorms help firm the flesh, develop the fruit sugars, and give these apples their incomparable flavor."

Nobody sent the apples back. And the next year the apple grower got orders with many notes expressing a preference for hail-marked apples rather than unblemished ones.

MANY GRIEVANCES demand that something be done, but many only require that we simply allow the complainer to vent his or her spleen.

In such cases we should follow the example of the wise old minister who kept a large book on the lectern in the church rectory. Emblazoned in big letters on the cover were the words *Member Complaints*.

Whenever members of his flock came to him with a complaint, he would listen intently and thank the person for bringing the matter to his attention. "This is one for the book," he would say as he walked the person to the rectory door. If the complainer glanced back, the minister could be seen, pen in hand, bent over the book.

When he finally went to his eternal reward, the church elders opened the book. Its pages were blank.

VETERAN AMERICAN LEAGUE baseball umpire Bill Guthrie was working behind the plate one afternoon and the catcher for the visiting team was repeatedly protesting his calls. Guthrie endured this for a number of innings, and then called a halt.

"Son," he said softly, "you've been a big help to me in calling balls and strikes today, and I appreciate it. But I think I've got the hang of it now, so I'm going to ask you to go to the clubhouse and show whoever's there how to take a shower."

A YOUNG COUPLE decided to start their own business. He was an engineer and she was an advertising copywriter. They wound up buying a small salmon cannery in Alaska. They soon discovered they had a problem. Customers opening a can of their salmon discovered that the fish was gray. Sales sagged.

Investigation revealed that the problem was a result of the way they processed the fish.

"This is a technical problem," said the wife, "and you're an engineer. You have to find a way to fix this."

A month later, the husband announced that they would have to replace some machinery and make other changes. It was going to take at least 10 months to do the job and it was going to cost a lot of money.

"We have to do something sooner than that," said the wife, "or we're going to go under."

For the next two days she pondered the problem and came up with this solution: There was nothing wrong with the salmon—it tasted fine. The problem lay in its looks. So she changed the label on the can. In bold letters, right under the brand name, the labels thereafter announced, "The only salmon guaranteed not to turn pink in the can."

TWO SONS were left a large piece of property by their father. For months they fought over how the land should be divided. Finally, they brought their problem to their rabbi and asked him to solve it.

"Come back tomorrow," said the rabbi, "and we'll talk."

The next day the sons returned and the rabbi gave them his solution.

"Toss a coin," he said to one of the brothers. "You call it, heads or tails," he said to the other. "The one who wins the toss, divides the land."

"That's no solution," said one of the brothers. "We're right back where we started from."

"Not so," said the rabbi. "The one who wins the toss divides the land; but the other gets first choice."

There are two ways we can meet a difficulty: either we can alter the difficulty or we can alter ourselves to meet it.

STRESS ❖ ❖ ❖

The time to relax is when you don't have the time for it.

WRITER CHARLES SWINDOLL once found himself with too many commitments in too few days. He got nervous and tense about it.

"I was snapping at my wife and our children, choking down my food at mealtimes, and feeling irritated at those unexpected interruptions through the day," he recalled in his book *Stress Fractures*. "Before long, things around our home started reflecting the patter of my hurry-up style. It was becoming unbearable.

"I distinctly remember after supper one evening, the words of our younger daughter, Colleen. She wanted to tell me something important that had happened to her at school that day. She began hurriedly, 'Daddy, I wanna tell you somethin' and I'll tell you really fast.'

"Suddenly realizing her frustration, I answered, 'Honey, you can tell me—and you don't have to tell me really fast. Say it slowly.'

"I'll never forget her answer: 'Then listen slowly.' "

❖ ❖ ❖ SUCCESS

I don't care what you do for a living. If you love it, you are a success.

GEORGE BURNS

"What is the secret of your success?" a reporter asked a bank president.

"Two words."

"And what would they be, sir?"

"Right decisions."

"And how do you make the right decisions?"

"Experience."

"And how do you get experience?"

"Two words."

"What are they?"

"Wrong decisions."

Some ingredients of success: to be able to carry money without spending it; to be able to bear an injustice without retaliating; to be able to keep on the job until it is finished; to be able to do one's duty even when one is not watched; to be able to accept criticism without letting it whip you.

Success is to be measured not so much by the position that one has reached in life as by the obstacles that one has overcome while trying to succeed.

BOOKER T. WASHINGTON

HERE'S A YOUNG GIRL who is destined to succeed:

She visited a farm one day and wanted to buy a large watermelon.

"That's three dollars," said the farmer.

"I've only got 30 cents," said the young girl.

The farmer pointed to a very small watermelon in the field and said, "How about that one?"

"Okay, I'll take it," said the little girl. "But leave it on the vine. I'll be back for it in a month."

The late James Burrill Angell, president of the University of Michigan for 38 years, was once asked for the secret of his success. "Grow antennae, not horns," he replied.

---

*What makes a truly successful executive is not intelligence, education, lifestyle, or background. The principal factor that determines an executive's success is his or her ability to deal with **people**.*

THERE'S a story about Moshe, a poor shoemaker who dies and finds himself about to meet his maker. He begins to make excuses about why he did not make more of himself in life.

With this he is warned, "When you are in His presence He will not ask you why you were not Moses or King David or one of the prophets. He will ask you why you were not Moshe the shoemaker."

We are not asked to be great. We are just asked to be all that we can be.

If you have lived well, laughed often, and loved much, consider yourself a success.

AN EXECUTIVE was asked what her formula for success was.

"It's very simple," she said. "Just 10 simple two-letter words:

"If it is to be, it is up to me."

AFTER ACTOR/DIRECTOR Michael Douglas had been in five blockbuster films, his father, actor Kirk Douglas, wrote him a note.

177

It said, "Michael, I'm more proud of how you *handle* success than I am of your success."

It's a note Michael Douglas treasures.

The Lord gave us two ends—one to sit on and the other to think with. Success depends on which one we use the most.

ANN LANDERS

SOMERSET MAUGHAM, the English writer, once wrote a story about a janitor at St. Peter's Church in London. One day a young vicar discovered that the janitor was illiterate and fired him.

Jobless, the man invested his meager savings in a tiny tobacco shop, where he prospered, bought another, expanded, and ended up with a chain of tobacco stores worth several hundred thousand dollars.

One day the man's banker said, "You've done well for an illiterate, but where would you be if you could read and write?"

"Well," replied the man, "I'd be janitor of St. Peter's Church in Neville Square."

The difference between a successful career and a mediocre one sometimes consists of leaving about four or five things a day unsaid.

THERE is a four-word formula for success that applies equally well to organizations or individuals: Make yourself more useful.

◈　◈　◈　**TACT**

To WELCOME its new minister, a congregation held a reception and a member presented him with a pie to take home. The pie turned out to be inedible and the minister's wife reluctantly put it in the garbage.

The next Sunday, the woman who baked the pie approached the minister after the service, and he felt compelled to make some comment.

"Thank you for being so kind and thoughtful last week," he said. "A pie like that never lasts long at our house."

The minister was using that marvelous thing called *tact*. Tact is kindness with brains. It's a way of putting your best foot forward without stepping on anyone's toes. It stems from the Latin word *tactus*, which means *touch*. It is a delicate, sensitive touch that works with human nature, not against it.

Many of us get a chance to use it every day—especially those who must deal with disagreeable and unreasonable customers. Be tactful and you'll put yourself on the road to success.

◈　◈　◈　**TAXES**

FORM 1040 could easily have been called 1039 or 1041. The IRS has assured the American public that the number 1040 was a random selection. Still, some taxpayers insist it's not a mere coincidence that in merry old England, Lady Godiva, dressed only in long hair, rode through Coventry protesting oppressive taxes *in the year 1040.*

It seems a little ridiculous now, but this country was originally founded as a protest against taxation.

IN a newly created nation in Africa, an elderly native was told that he was going to be taxed to support the government.

"Why?" he asked.

"To protect you from enemies, to feed you when you are hungry, to care for you when you are sick, and to educate your children," he was told.

"I see," said the old man. "It's like I have this dog, and the dog is hungry. He comes begging to me for food. So I take my knife, cut off a piece of the poor dog's tail, and give it to him to eat. That, I believe, is what this taxation is."

TEAMWORK ❖ ❖ ❖

BEES can show you something about teamwork. On a warm day about half the bees in a hive stay inside beating their wings while the other half go out to gather pollen and nectar. Because of the beating wings, the temperature inside the hive is about 10 degrees cooler than outside. The bees rotate duties and the bees that cool the hive one day are honey gatherers the next.

Team spirit is what gives so many companies an edge over their competitors.

GEORGE L. CLEMENTS

THERE'S A LESSON in the legend about a herd of mules that were being attacked nightly by a pack of wolves.

When the wolves arrived each night, the mules would begin braying and kicking in all directions. As a result, the mules injured and maimed each other. The agile wolves were unharmed.

After several of these night raids, a wise mule figured out how to deal with the problem. He called all the mules together and told them about it.

That night, the wolves came slinking out of the nearby woods as usual and attacked. But this time the mules put their heads together in a circle and began kicking outward. The wolves were dispersed and the mules did no harm to each other.

It is better to have one person working with you than three people working for you.

❖ ❖ ❖ **TEMPER**

EDWIN STANTON, secretary of war under Lincoln, was well known for a highly inflammable temper. The pressure of war kept his nerves frayed and his tongue sharp. Once, when he complained to Lincoln about a certain general, Lincoln told him to write the man a letter. "Tell him off," Lincoln advised.

Stanton, bolstered by the President's support, promptly wrote a scathing letter in which he tore the man to shreds. He showed the letter to the President. "Good," said Lincoln, "first rate. You certainly gave it to him."

As Stanton started to leave, Lincoln asked, "What are you going to do with it now?"

"Mail it, of course," said Stanton.

"Nonsense," snorted the President, "you don't want to send that letter. Put it in the stove! That's what I do when I have written a letter while I'm angry. You had a good time writing that letter. Now forget about it."

THINKING ❖ ❖ ❖

Thinking is the hardest work there is, which is probably the reason why so few engage in it.

HENRY FORD

A MAN had bought his daughter a bicycle—unassembled, of course—and after reading and rereading the instructions he couldn't figure out how it went together. Finally, he sought the help of an old handyman who was working in the backyard.

The old fellow picked up the pieces, studied them, then began assembling the bicycle. In a short time, he had put it together. "That's amazing," said the man. "And you did it without even looking at the instructions!"

"Fact is," said the old man, "I can't read and when a fellow can't read, he's got to think."

EDWARD DE BONO, the Oxford exponent of lateral thinking, suggests that when we can't solve a problem using traditional methods, we should try "detours and reversals," anything that will give us a different angle from which to ponder solutions. To illustrate, he tells this story about a problem faced by executives of a large company:

The company had moved into a new skyscraper and discovered that the builder apparently had not put in enough elevators. Employees were disgruntled because there were overlong waits for elevators, especially at both ends of the working day.

The company got a wide cross section of the staff together and asked them to sit down and solve the problem. The task force came up with four possible solutions:

1. Speed up the elevators, or arrange for them to stop at certain floors during rush periods.

2. Stagger working hours to reduce elevator demand at either end of the day.

3. Install mirrors around entrances to all elevators.

4. Drive a new elevator shaft through the building.

Which solution would *you* have chosen?

According to Professor de Bono, if you chose the first, second, or fourth solutions, then you are a "vertical" or traditional thinker. If you chose the third possibility, then you are a "lateral thinker." The vertical thinker takes the narrow view; the lateral thinker has a broader view.

After some consideration, the company chose the third solution. It worked.

"People became so preoccupied with looking at themselves (or surreptitiously at others)," said de Bono, "that they no longer noticed the wait for the elevator. The problem was not so much the lack of elevators as the impatience of the employees."

———————

THOUGHTFULNESS ❖ ❖ ❖

THE SPACIOUS roadside park adjacent to an interstate highway contained attractive picnic areas, convenient drinking fountains, and clean rest room facilities. The Texas Highway Department obviously had thought of everything, including appropriate accommodations for travel-weary pets: two bright red fireplugs.

Thoughtfulness comes in many forms, and it is virtually always welcomed by its recipients. Thoughtfulness is a habit—a way of life well worth cultivating and practicing.

The thoughtful person is quick to pay a well-deserved compliment, or to send a prompt note of congratulations to someone who has received a promotion, an honor, or special recognition.

Thoughtful people park a bit farther from the entrance of the store or the post office, leaving the nearer space for someone who doesn't get around as easily as they once did.

The thoughtful person takes photographs of his neighbors' homes after a beautiful snowfall, and later surprises those friends with the cherished snapshots.

Thoughtful people don't wait for opportunities—they imaginatively create numerous opportunities to make life brighter, smoother, and more enjoyable for those about them.

Our thoughtful attitudes and generous deeds can make many people happy—including ourselves.

WILLIAM A. WARD

❖ ❖ ❖ **TIME**

TIME is the one thing we all possess. Our success depends on the proper use of our time and its by-product, the odd moment.

Every minute that you save by making it useful or more profitable is that much added to your life and its possibilities. Every minute lost is a neglected by-product—once gone, you will never get it back.

Think of the odd quarter of an hour before breakfast, the odd half hour after lunch. Remember the chance to read, or figure, or think with concentration about your own career, that presents itself now and again during the day. All these opportunities are the by-products of your daily existence. Use them and you may find what many successful companies have found—that the real profit is in the utilization of the by-products.

Among the aimless, unsuccessful, or worthless, you often hear talk about "killing time." Those who are always killing time are really killing their own chances in life. Those who are destined to become successful are those who make time live by making it useful.

ARTHUR BRISBANE

Make each day useful and cheerful and prove that you know the worth of time by employing it well. Then youth will be happy, elders will be without regret, and life will be a beautiful success.

LOUISA MAY ALCOTT

HENRY FORD was always dropping into the offices of the executives of his company. When asked why he didn't have them come to him, he said, "Well, I'll tell you. I've found that I can leave the

185

other fellow's office a lot quicker than I can get him to leave mine."

You will never *find* time for anything. If you want time you must *make* it.

CHARLES BUXTON

BENJAMIN FRANKLIN was putting out a newspaper in Philadelphia when someone came into the office of his publishing company where there were some booklets and pamphlets by Franklin for sale.

The customer browsed around and finally picked up a book and asked an assistant how much it cost.

"One dollar," said the assistant.

The customer demurred. "Couldn't you come down a little?" he asked.

"I'm sorry," said the assistant, "the price of the book is a dollar."

The customer demanded to see Mr. Franklin. Franklin was in the middle of putting out the newspaper, but that didn't seem to bother the customer. He asked Franklin if he could bring the price of the book down.

"The book," said Franklin, "costs one dollar and a quarter."

Taken by surprise, the customer said, "But your assistant only asked a dollar."

"If you had bought it at that price," said Franklin, "I would honor that price. But you have taken me away from my regular duties."

The customer did not give up. "Come on, Mr. Franklin, what is the lowest price you can take for this book?"

"One dollar and a half," said Franklin. "And the more this haggling goes on, the more you are taking up my time and the more I must charge you."

The customer had learned an old lesson: Time is money.

If it weren't for the last minute, very little would get done.

❖ ❖ ❖ **TIPPING**

HUMORIST ROBERT BENCHLEY was usually a generous tipper, but on one occasion he decided not to tip anyone at the resort hotel he was leaving because the service had been so bad. He pointedly ignored all the hotel employees lined up expectantly, until he reached the final barrier—the doorman.

"You're not going to forget me, are you, sir?" the doorman said, holding out his hand.

Benchley grasped the outstretched hand and shook it. "No," he said, "I'll write to you."

IN THE DAYS when an ice cream sundae cost much less, a 10-year-old boy entered a hotel coffee shop and sat at a table. A waitress put a glass of water in front of him. "How much is an ice cream sundae?"

"Fifty cents," replied the waitress.

The little boy pulled his hand out of his pocket and studied a number of coins in it. "How much is a dish of plain ice cream?" he inquired.

Some people were now waiting for a table and the waitress was a bit impatient. "Thirty-five cents," she said brusquely.

The little boy again counted the coins. "I'll have the plain ice cream," he said.

The waitress brought the ice cream, put the bill on the table, and walked away. The boy finished the ice cream, paid the cashier, and departed. When the waitress came back, she picked up the empty plate and then swallowed hard at what she saw. There, placed neatly beside the empty dish, were two nickels and five pennies—her tip.

WE DON'T really believe it, but we know a fellow who claims that he has discovered a foolproof method of getting good service in restaurants. He says he asks for a small bowl and puts two dimes in it. Then he props a card up against it. Printed on the card in letters large enough for the waiter to read is this message: *Your Tip So Far.*

UNDERSTANDING ❖ ❖ ❖

THERE'S A WONDERFUL STORY from the book *Zadig* by the immortal Voltaire.

The ruler of an important country was distraught. His favorite horse, a spirited charger, was missing. The king sent couriers throughout the land looking for it, but to no avail. The horse had disappeared.

In desperation, the king offered a large sum for its return. This too failed. The days went by and no one had an inkling about where the horse—dead or alive—was.

In the king's court was a simple soul, not even bright enough to be a court jester. He gained an audience with the king and told him that he could find the lost horse.

"*You!* You can find my horse?" exclaimed the king. "You say you can find my horse when the best and brightest of men in my realm have failed?"

"I can, sir," said the simpleton.

The king had nothing to lose. An all-out effort to find the horse had been made without success, so the king told the simpleton to see what he could do.

Within hours the horse was tethered in front of the royal palace. When the king saw it, he was ecstatic. He was astounded. He was thankful! He immediately issued a large reward to his simple-minded servant and insisted on an explanation of how the horse had been found.

"Why, sire, 'twas very easy, very easy indeed," said the simpleton. "I merely put myself in your horse's place and asked myself where I would have gone were I a horse. I went there. And there was your horse."

It was a matter of viewpoint. The simpleton put himself in the horse's place. In doing so, he could better understand how the horse's thought process worked.

The same process can work for you, in or out of the workplace. An old Indian adage asks us to walk a mile in another's moccasins when trying to understand him. It's a simple piece of advice that anyone can use. Follow it and you'll have much less trouble getting on in this world.

UNEMPLOYMENT ❖ ❖ ❖

LOSS OF A JOB may not be as bad as it seems. It might point you in a new direction. It may cause you to assess your performance and try to improve it. If your company got gobbled up by a conglomerate, if it "downsized," if it moved, or closed down, that's not your fault. Whatever the reason, only your job has ended. *You* haven't.

A FORMER executive of a company that had been taken over in a corporate merger gave this description of what had happened to his company's executive personnel: "We got the mushroom treatment. Right after the acquisition, we were left in the dark. Then they covered us with manure. After that they let us stew for a while. Finally, they canned us."

ISADORE BARMASH

VISION ❖ ❖ ❖

AN INDIAN CHIEF used to try the strength of the young men in his tribe by making them run, without stopping, as far up a mountain as they could.

One day, four young braves competed. The first returned with a branch of spruce, indicating how far up the mountain he had gone. The second came back with a pine twig, showing that he had gone farther. The third brought back a branch of an Alpine shrub.

The afternoon passed, the sun went down, and the fourth brave had not returned. Finally, by the light of the moon, he made his way back. He was exhausted and his feet were bloody.

"How high did you go and what did you bring?" asked the chief.

"Where I went," said the brave, "there was neither spruce nor pine to shelter me from the sun, no flowers to cheer the way, no shrubs to impede the path, but only barren land and snow and rocks. My feet are torn and I am weary and late, but"—and as a wonderful light came into his eyes, he added—"I saw the sea."

◊ ◊ ◊ **WEALTH**

There are two ways you can be rich. One is to have all you want, the other is to be satisfied with what you have.

YOUNG PEOPLE will not remember, but when radio ruled the airwaves, there was a popular program called *The Goldbergs*.

In one episode, Jake Goldberg came home for supper and excitedly told his wife, Molly, about a great idea he had. He wanted to go into business. Molly had some money put away, anticipating just such a thing, and she gave it to him.

As they sat at the dinner table, enthusiastically discussing the future, Jake said, "Molly, some day we'll be eating off golden plates!"

Molly looked at him and replied, "Jake, darling, will it taste any better?"

Young people don't have to remember *The Goldbergs*, but they *should* remember that line.

If you've saved a lot of money in your life, you may be rich. If

you've saved a lot of heartache for others, there's no question about it—you're rich.

There are two things needed in these days: first, for rich people to find out how poor people live; and second, for poor people to know how rich people work.

JOHN FOSTER

A YOUNG STOCKBROKER had a particularly successful year on Wall Street and to celebrate he bought himself a modest yacht.

One day he took his grandmother to see the boat. While they were touring it he put on a cap that sported gold braid and crossed anchors. "See," he said, "I'm the captain."

The grandmother made no comment and the young man remarked, "You don't seem very impressed."

"You want me to be impressed?" said the grandmother. "So okay, I'll be impressed. To yourself, you're a captain. To me, you're maybe a captain. But to captains, you're no captain."

WISDOM ❖ ❖ ❖

MUCH wisdom can be crowded into but four words:

In God we trust. This too shall pass. Live and let live. Still waters run deep. Bad news travels fast. Love laughs at locksmiths. Nothing succeeds like success. Charity begins at home. Politics make strange bedfellows. Nothing ventured, nothing gained. Man proposes, God disposes. Let sleeping dogs lie.

THREE MEN set out on a journey. Each carried two sacks around his neck—one in front and one in back. Which of them finished first?

The first man was asked what was in his sacks. "In this one on my back," he said, "I carry all the kind deeds of my friends. In that way they are out of sight and out of mind and I don't have to do anything about them. They're soon forgotten. This sack in front carries all the unkind things people do to me. I pause in my journey every day and take these out to study. It slows me down, but nobody gets away with anything."

The second man said he kept his own good deeds in his front sack. "I constantly keep them before me," he said. "It gives me pleasure to take them out and air them."

"The sack on your back seems heavy," someone remarked. "What's in it?"

"Merely my little mistakes," said the second man. "I always keep them on my back."

The third man was asked what he kept in *his* sacks.

"I carry my friends' kind deeds in this front sack," he said.

"It looks full. It must be heavy," said an observer.

"No," said the third man, "it is big, but not heavy. Far from being a burden, it is like the sails of a ship. It helps me move ahead."

"I notice that the sack behind you has a hole in the bottom," said the observer. "It seems empty and of very little use."

"That's where I put all the evil I hear from others," said the third man. "It just falls out and is lost, so I have no weight to impede me."

———————————

IT IS HARD: to forget, to apologize, to save money, to be unselfish, to avoid mistakes, to keep out of a rut, to begin all over again, to

193

make the best of all things, to keep your temper at all times, to think first and act afterward, to maintain a high standard, to keep on keeping on, to shoulder the blame, to be charitable, to admit error, to take advice, to forgive. *But it pays!*

Watch your thoughts; they become words.
Watch your words; they become actions.
Watch your actions; they become habits.
Watch your habits; they become character.
Watch your character; it becomes your destiny.

FRANK OUTLAW

In the midst of great joy do not promise anyone anything. In the midst of great anger do not answer anyone's letter.

CHINESE PROVERB

Any faucet can turn the water on, but after a few years only a good faucet will turn it off. The same thing applies to human tongues.

WHAT YOU SPEND YEARS BUILDING may be destroyed overnight. Build anyway.

The good you do today may not be remembered tomorrow. Do good anyway.

Honesty and frankness may make you vulnerable to attack. Be honest anyway.

People who need help can be confused and distressed, and they may attack you when you try to help. Help them anyway.

People are unreasonable, illogical, and self-centered. Try to love them anyway.

If you are successful, you may win false friends and true enemies. Succeed anyway.

Be wiser than other people, if you can, but do not tell them.

LORD CHESTERFIELD

To *look* is one thing.
To *see* what you look at is another.
To *understand* what you see is a third.
To *learn* from what you understand is still something else.
But to *act* on what you learn is all that really matters.

The only people with whom you should try to get even are those who have helped you.

MAE MALOO

If you're going to give someone a piece of your mind, make sure you can spare it.

If a thing goes without saying, then let it.

AN EXECUTIVE woke up one day to discover that it was 15 degrees outside, snowing, and windy.

She prayed for the good Lord to send her the strength to get up, get dressed, and jog 10 miles. Then she rolled over and went back to sleep. Instead of strength, the Lord had sent her wisdom.

WOMEN ❖ ❖ ❖

A FELLOW walked into a bookstore and asked the woman behind the counter, "Have you got a book called, *Man, the Master of Women?*"

"Try the fiction section," said the woman.

––––––––––––

THERE'S A CHARMING STORY that Thomas Wheeler, CEO of the Massachusetts Mutual Life Insurance Company, told on himself.

He and his wife were driving along an interstate highway when he noticed that their car was low on gas. Wheeler got off the highway at the next exit and soon found a run-down gas station with just one gas pump. He asked the lone attendant to fill the tank and check the oil, then went for a little walk around the station to stretch his legs.

As he was returning to the car, he noticed that the attendant and his wife were engaged in an animated conversation. The conversation stopped as he paid the attendant. But as he was getting back into the car, he saw the attendant wave and heard him say, "It was great talking to you."

As they drove out of the station, Wheeler asked his wife if she knew the man. She readily admitted she did. They had gone to high school together and had dated steadily for about a year.

"Boy, were you lucky that I came along," bragged Wheeler. "If you had married him, you'd be the wife of a gas station attendant instead of the wife of a chief executive officer."

"My dear," replied his wife, "if I had married him, he'd be the chief executive officer and you'd be the gas station attendant."

Women have more imagination than men. They need it to tell us how wonderful we are.

ARNOLD H. GLASGOW

❖ ❖ ❖ **WORK**

Don't watch the clock. Do what it does. Keep going.

SAM LEVENSON

WANTED: People for hard work, people who can find things to be done without the help of a manager and three assistants.

People who get to work on time and do not imperil the lives of others in an attempt to be the first off the job each day.

People who listen carefully when they are spoken to and ask only enough questions to ensure the accurate carrying out of instructions.

People who look you straight in the eye and tell the truth every time.

People who do not sulk about an hour's overtime in emergencies.

People who are cheerful and courteous to everyone, and determined to make good.

These people are wanted everywhere. Age or lack of experience does not count. There isn't any limit, except their own ambitions, to the number or size of the jobs they can get. They are wanted in every business.

———

My grandfather once told me that there are two kinds of people: those who do the work and those who take the credit. He told me to try to be in the first group; there was less competition there.

INDIRA GANDHI

———

A WOMAN advertised for someone to work in her garden, and two men applied for the job. She was interviewing them out on the front lawn when she noticed her mother, on the porch, making signs to her to choose the shorter man, which she did.

"But I liked the taller fellow's face. It was a strong face."

"Face!" exclaimed the mother. "When you're hiring somebody to work in your garden, look at his pants! If the knees are worn or patched, you hire him. If they're worn or patched on the seat, you don't."

———

If you love your work, you're likely to be its master; if you hate it, it's *your* master.

———

SOMEBODY ONCE SAID that the only one who got everything done by Friday was Robinson Crusoe.

Friday, of course, was Crusoe's servant. The other Friday—the last day of the workweek—is no one's servant. Many of us are appalled at how much work remains come Friday afternoon.

If you have the same problem, take heart. There's a relatively simple way to deal with it. Just follow this advice from professional time-study researchers:

Get up 15 minutes earlier to avoid the morning rush. Early in his career, Dwight Eisenhower streamlined the procedure for getting up, shaving, bathing, and having breakfast. He decided the night before what he was going to wear the next day and thus eliminated a lot of fumbling around in the morning. He always arrived on the job feeling relaxed.

List the day's tasks and do them in order of importance. Many successful people fix in their minds a list of duties and appointments for the day, and go over them while getting ready in the morning.

Pinpoint your goal. A lot of people waste time and energy on a job simply because they lack a clear idea of what they want to do or what they are supposed to do.

Take a step at a time. Those who conquer mountains literally inch their way to the summits. In the same way, by whittling your major goal down to a series of minor steps, you'll simplify the task at hand.

Work rapidly. Tests show that the rapid worker is usually more accurate than the slow, *steady* one. This may be because the rapid worker usually tries out different speeds of working and finds the one that is most effective. The slow worker never really finds what he or she can do.

Set deadlines and see whether you can beat them. This provides extra incentive and may actually increase your efficiency. What's more, you are being affirmative when you set up time limits for yourself. When you say to yourself, "I know I can do this job by a certain time," the chances are you'll do it.

Do these things and you'll get things done. Time will no longer be your enemy and your weekends will be more enjoyable.

———————

JULIA CHILD was in the middle of one of her TV cooking programs when she lifted two lids from steaming pans and clanged them together exuberantly over her head, like cymbals. Condensed water from the lids showered down on her and all over the front of her blouse. She nonchalantly wiped her front with a towel and said laughingly, "I don't know why I did that. It was silly!" Ah! If only we all could find such joy in our work!

Find something you love to do and you'll never have to work a day in your life.

HARVEY MACKAY

IF A MAN is called to be a streetsweeper, he should sweep streets even as Michelangelo painted, or Beethoven composed music, or Shakespeare wrote poetry.

He should sweep streets so well that all the hosts of heaven and earth will pause to say, here lived a great streetsweeper who did his job well.

MARTIN LUTHER KING, JR.

The highest reward for a person's toil is not what they get for it, but what they become by it.

JOHN RUSKIN

SMITH DIED and regained consciousness in the next world. He looked out over a vast expanse of pleasant country. After resting comfortably for a while in a delightful spot, he began to get a little bored. He called out, "Is there anybody here?"

An attendant, appropriately dressed in white, appeared and said gravely, "What do you want?"

"What can I have?" asked Smith.

"Whatever you want."

"May I have something to eat?"

They brought him delicious dishes, even the things he liked best on earth. Smith was having a wonderful time eating, sleeping, and calling for more good things.

But presently he wanted something more. He called for games. They came in profusion. Then he called for books and read with excitement and pleasure. He called for anything that struck his fancy and received it in abundant measure. But at last the boredom caught up with him, and he shouted, "I want something to *do*!"

The attendant appeared and said, "I am sorry, but that is the only thing we cannot give you here."

By this time Smith was frantic for something to do and in his terrible frustration cried out, "I'm sick and tired of everything here; I'd rather go to hell!"

"Where do you think you are?" asked the attendant.

❖ ❖ ❖ WORKING COUPLES

THE WIFE of a statistician, determined to find a job, cajoled her husband into staying home for a day to take care of their children.

When she returned, he handed her the following report: dried tears, nine times; tied shoes, 13 times; toy balloons purchased, 16; average life of balloon, 10 seconds; cautioned children not to cross street, 21 times; number of times children crossed street, 21. Number of times I will do this again, zero.

MARY WAS MARRIED to a male chauvinist. They both worked full time, but he never did anything around the house and certainly not any housework. *That,* he declared, was woman's work.

But one evening Mary arrived home from work to find the children bathed, a load of wash in the washing machine and another in the dryer, dinner on the stove, and a beautifully set table, complete with flowers.

She was astonished, and she immediately wanted to know what was going on. It turned out that Charley, her husband, had read a magazine article that suggested working wives would be more romantically inclined if they weren't so tired from having to do all the housework in addition to holding down a full-time job.

The next day, she couldn't wait to tell her friends in the office.

"How did it work out?" one of them asked.

"Well, it was a great dinner," Mary said. "Charley even cleaned up, helped the kids with their homework, folded the laundry, and put everything away."

"But what about afterward?" her friends wanted to know.

"It didn't work out," Mary said. "Charley was too tired."

WE HEARD about a lovely ritual a working couple and their little daughter go through every workday.

When the mother or father leaves the child at a day-care center each morning, he or she kisses the palm of the child's hand and the child reciprocates. Then they both close their hands tightly and put the "kisses" in their pockets.

If the little girl gets lonely during the day, she can put her hand into her pocket, take out the kiss, and put it on her cheek. That makes things easier until one of her parents shows up at the end of the workday.

♦ ♦ ♦ **WORRY**

A day of worry is more exhausting than a week of work.

Worry does not empty tomorrow of its sorrow; it empties today of its strength.

CORRIE TEN BOOM

Half the worry in the world is caused by people trying to make decisions before they have sufficient knowledge on which to base a decision.

DEAN HAWKES

GROVE PATTERSON, editor of the *Toledo Blade* many years ago, always thought that the slang expression, *So what?*, had real value.

"I have an idea," Patterson once wrote, "that we can apply it to about 50 percent of our troubles, and find that it is a comfortable cure-all.

"I know a so-called big industrialist who is forever worrying about trivialities," said Patterson. "He is constantly engaged in postmortems. The right answer, which he doesn't know, to practically all his fulminations is *So what?*

"I am the frequent victim of my own postmortems," said Patterson. "I sometimes lie awake nights trying to figure out why I did this or that, or didn't do it, and all the time the easy conclusion is within my grasp: *So what?*

"Many of us complain because of our lot in life when it is evident that there is little we can do about it. *So what?* We didn't ask to be born, but here we are. *So what?* Others complain about circumstances which they could change if they had the courage and the energy. These people really don't have much use for this phrase. I speak mostly of and for those who seek to repour the water that has gone under the bridge. When we finally come to learn that many things come to all of us that we cannot do anything about, we shall have put a broad and sturdy plank into the foundation of our philosophy."

WRITING ❖ ❖ ❖

BRUCE BARTON, who made a name for himself years ago as a writer and advertising man, was talking to a class of students about writing one evening. One of them asked him how he got his inspiration for his magazine articles.

"Well," Barton replied, "picture me sitting at breakfast in the morning. As I sip my coffee, my wife glances down at the floor and observes, 'Bruce, we really need a new dining room rug. This one is wearing out.' Right there I have the inspiration to write another article."

———

WHY DON'T people write better letters and reports? The biggest stumbling block, believe it or not, isn't a matter of technique or writing ability. It's a matter of mental attitude. The reason most people don't write better is because they are too self-centered. Self-centeredness is the curse of good writing.

In writing of any kind the important thing is to plant an idea in the reader's mind or to stimulate feelings or emotions. In all good writing, one person and only one person is important—the reader. Yet what happens when the average person sits down to write a letter or report? Somewhere in his or her conscious or unconscious mind an insidious thought raises its head: *What will the reader think of me?* The more that thought interferes with concentrating on the reader, the poorer the writing will be.

Why do so many executives, lawyers, scientists, and engineers sound like executives, lawyers, scientists, and engineers in everything they write? Because they wouldn't want people to think of them in any other way. They're more concerned with the impression they're making than they are about the message.

And what happens when an executive comes along who isn't trying to impress anybody, who's just trying to get his or her ideas across in the simplest, clearest fashion to the reader? More often than not, this person impresses far more than those who are striving to be impressive.

Perhaps you work for the largest, most powerful organization in the world. If so, when you start to write or dictate, forget it! Your corporation consists of pleasant, friendly people. So get politely to the point, wrap it up, and wish your correspondent well. Write to him or her in the same language you would use if you were carrying on a conversation across the desk. "Stay loose!" as my old baseball coach used to say.

JOHN L. BECKLEY
The Power of Little Words

INDEX